BETTER
JUMPING

BETTER JUMPING

Using Grid Work for Success at Every Level

CAROL MAILER

J.A. ALLEN · LONDON

© Carol Mailer 2008
First published in Great Britain 2008

ISBN 978 0 85131 949 0

J.A. Allen
Clerkenwell House
Clerkenwell Green
London ECIR OHT

J.A. Allen is an imprint of Robert Hale Limited

www.halebooks.com

The right of Carol Mailer to be identified as author of this work has been asserted
by her in accordance with the Copyright, Designs and Patents Act 1988

A catalogue record for this book is available from the British Library

Photography by Matthew Roberts
Design and typesetting by Paul Saunders
Edited by Jane Lake
Grid diagrams by Rodney Paull

Printed in China
and arranged by New Era Printing Co. Limited, Hong Kong

Contents

Acknowledgements

My thanks to all the riders shown in *Better Jumping* who were as enthusiastic for the unflattering shots to be used as well as the good ones. Thank you to Jo Naylor, Reiko Anderson, Donna Rawlinson and the Pryke family for their help with setting up the grids and courses I wanted to use, and to Allison Lowther who transcribed my dictaphone ramblings at the photo sessions and noted everything down for later reference. Thanks to Lorraine Jones for her enthusiasm in organizing and putting on a show specifically for my riders and me.

And my thanks of course to Matthew Roberts who read my mind and unfailingly captured with his camera exactly the right moment in time to illustrate all the different situations and methods I wanted to show.

Introduction

Whatever level of riding you attain, however competent or experienced you are and however many competitions you win, you will always want to improve your jumping. Whether you are a complete beginner or competing at the highest level, there is always more you can do to further your skills and you will discover that you need never stop learning how to achieve better jumping. As in most sport, wanting to do better is almost irresistible, and improvement will probably be your main aim.

Grid work is the key, it provides: the building blocks to help you improve; the steps and stages to competence; enjoyment and safety. You would not expect to be able to read if you didn't learn the alphabet, and so how can you expect to begin jumping or improve your jumping skills, which the use of grids will encourage and develop, without this basic and repetitious work.

If you are a 'happy hacker', wouldn't it be fun to just pop over the occasional small log, rail or ditch when you are riding out? And wouldn't it be *more* fun to do it comfortably and competently, minimizing any risk to you and your horse?

If you become a little more ambitious once you have discovered the sheer fun of jumping, you might want to try something a bit more demanding: a local show, hunter trial, or one-day event perhaps. If you are keen to be competitive, you shouldn't have to look too far to find a show that is suitable to start off with. The jumps usually get progressively larger class by class as the day goes on, and so you will always be able to study jumps that are higher and wider and combinations that are more difficult than a simple double of uprights. Even if you aren't ready to go up to the next class on a particular day, you will be able to walk the course and recognize what sort of grids you should be practising at home to enable the move up to the next class to be straightforward. And there are always shows with more difficult classes, something more challenging to aim at.

If you are at the stage of winning classes at around the 1.10 or 1.20 height courses, the grid work will help you become even more proficient and ready to tackle even bigger tracks and compete on equal terms with more experienced and professional riders. You don't want to enter a class and be out of your depth, looking like an amateur who doesn't belong in the same ring as the other competitors. Confidence can be very fragile when you move up a grade and it would be easy to regret being bold if your resulting efforts are disappointing.

Top international riders will only enter a class if they know they have a good chance of success, otherwise they would be wasting their entrance fees and putting extra unnecessary mileage on a good horse. The rider who is most successful in the class – the rider who wins – is the one who on that particular day jumps a little better than his rivals. All the horses at that level are more than capable of scooping up the top prize; they would not be entered if they weren't, and so it is the rider who is most in tune with his horse, the rider who is most consistent the whole way round, the rider who makes fewer mistakes on that day who will come out on top.

The other riders will just wish that they had been a little more positive, re-balanced a little quicker, turned a little shorter, and jumped a little better. There is *always* room for improvement, however good you are.

There is so much you can do at home to practise and improve, to develop your skills to get the most satisfaction out of your jumping efforts.

Grid work will give you everything you need to help you jump better, to literally go up to the next level. If you are keen to improve, the right sort of grid and the methodical approach to the exercises will encourage and produce a far better understanding of how to physically and mentally make jumping easy and enjoyable for your horse as well as you.

Grids will improve the jumping of any and every horse and rider without fail but they must be built to encourage both horse and rider to do better in logical stages, not to be tried and used as quick fixes. Occasionally, a new rider comes to me for training and tells me categorically that their horse won't or can't do grid work. Obviously the wrong methods and possibly the wrong distances have been used ensuring that both the rider and the horse have got in a right muddle. Perhaps students think I can wave a magic wand to turn riders and their horses into jumping machines without any effort, but I can't. Going back to basics, however,

will work every time, even if they have to start with one set of cross poles on its own, gradually introducing more to the grid as the horse starts to find the work easy.

So many riders find that their horse is not responding to the work as well as they had hoped and give up far too quickly. They want to change the grid before the horse is established and confident, or try to improve the way of going by bullying the horse or they try too hard to have a positive effect.

I find it difficult to have endless patience when a horse goes down a grid and kicks poles out everywhere because I'm the one who has to pick them up and reset them, but I have learned over a very long time that the *only* way to get a result is to be persistent and consistent. I try very hard to remain encouraging, especially when the rider is convinced that it won't work, but I am very secure in the knowledge that the grids *will* do the job. The rider just has to recognize that it may be a longer-term project than they hoped for.

There is no quick route to jumping better. Sheer hard work and repetition at every stage will produce the improvement you hope for, but it will be a gradual process. You need to be aware when you embark on your series of exercises that the variety and make up of the grids suggested will always help you jump better, from basic beginner grids right through to remedial speed grids and figure-of-eight formats. The subtle adjustment – by inches rather than feet – to the canter poles suggested for use with the grids will also make a world of difference. In the right place, they will help you recognize just how much you need to do to produce the best results, how quickly you need to land from a fence and rebalance your power and speed to get the up-tempo canter which will give you the best shot at your next jump.

There is no doubt that the progressive nature of

the exercises suggested will bring out the potential ability of both horse and rider. If you miscalculate how well things are going and you do encounter a problem when you move on to the next exercise, there is such a simple remedy. Just go back one or two stages to the earlier work and stay in that comfort zone, whether this is for the benefit of you, the horse or both of you, until you are happy and confident enough to move on again.

This is where a decent trainer, someone on the ground you can trust, will be such a help. They will know instinctively when it would be better to repeat stages, and the decision will be taken from you. You must not feel that you have lost face or been wimpy by going back a stage or two just because you are lacking confidence. It's a common-sense approach, but it's hard to acknowledge that you might have been wrong and a little too pushy, and actually caused the problem by being too ambitious. You don't want to persist in doing the wrong thing, when it is so easy to remedy, just because you feel you shouldn't backtrack. No harm will have been done and, most importantly, your trainer will know when you are ready to give the next exercise another go.

The grid work will *always* help. The only variable for each combination of horse and rider is the actual timescale it will take to achieve as much as you hope for. Don't set yourself a timetable. You might zip through some of the earlier exercises and then get stuck on something you would think should be quite simple. Or it might take several sessions to actually get down a very basic starter grid. Just aim to work at it methodically, and let the timescale take care of itself. You will see the sense in this when you try a more difficult exercise and get it right first time. And of course, there is always more to aim for, more grids to help you improve and more grids to make jumping better a foregone conclusion, not just a vague hope for the future.

All trainers tend to develop their own terms and expressions for certain things and where my terms appear throughout the book, I thought it best to give them a blanket explanation here.

I use the term **cross** or **crosses** when I am talking about cross poles; I have found that when teaching it is much simpler and quicker to use the abbreviated term.

Keep hold means the contact on the rein should be maintained without it becoming erratic or changing the feel on the horse's mouth.

Keep hold to the jump means definitely not changing the degree or strength of contact at the take-off point.

Hold is used to reaffirm and encourage the rider to maintain control and not to leave the horse, even for a split second, without the brakes, if necessary, or the steering.

Hold more outside rein means the outside rein should be held more strongly than the inside rein to maintain the steering and impulsion, as more use of the rider's inside leg into a supportive outside rein will encourage the horse's inside hind leg to come a little further underneath him to improve the strength, consistency and power of his impulsion.

More hold means a stronger feel or contact through the reins to the horse's mouth.

Soften your hold means that the rider should ease the strength of the contact with the horse's mouth very slightly without giving it away completely.

1 The horse, tack, clothes, accessories and jumps

No matter what horse you ride or how experienced you are, the grid work detailed in this book will help you jump better, but there are so many options to be considered before you even get on the horse. How you equip your horse and yourself will have a direct influence on the way you improve your jumping skills, as it will be difficult to make significant improvement without the right kit to help you both raise your standards. The kit doesn't need to be overly expensive or difficult to obtain, but the right or wrong choice will either help or hinder your progress.

The horse

Whether you own a horse already, or intend to practise with a borrowed or hired horse, the principles remain the same. The more you practise using the right methods, the more your jumping abilities and those of the horse will improve.

If you are a complete novice as far as jumping goes, a more experienced, willing, accomplished and genuine horse would be the best one to learn on. If he is forgiving and straightforward, you won't have to worry too much about being perfect and it will give you a chance to develop your own balance and rhythm without having to worry about him. Genuine schoolmasters are worth their weight in gold, and you'll be very fortunate if you can start off your jumping exercises with such an animal.

If you are a novice rider with a totally novice horse, the ideal preparation would be for a more experienced rider to start him off so that the rudiments of jumping are established before you take over. It would be difficult for the early stages of a horse's jumping education to be methodical and trouble free if the rider is uncertain about the help the horse will need. The horse does not deserve to have a difficult time as he learns purely because you don't know enough about what you are doing.

If you are a more practised rider, you will enjoy bringing on or improving any standard of horse from novice through to the more advanced stages, and all of the exercises suggested will give you better results.

Tack

Once you have your horse organized, you will need to kit him out ready for jumping as safely and sensibly as possible (Figure 1.1). Don't neglect any little detail concerning your horse's equipment, and don't adopt a casual attitude about using the full kit every time you jump. You would be so upset if an avoidable problem occurred simply because you were careless about remembering his boots or using a martingale, for example.

Tack safety

Your tack must fit the pair of you well and, primarily, be of a high enough standard to be as safe as

Figure 1.1 Bertie and Donna are kitted out smartly and safely for schooling. Bertie wears boots, stud-guard girth, martingale/breastplate, bridging reins and studs, and the saddle is furnished with safety stirrups. Donna wears plastic-tipped spurs, hat, gloves and a body protector under her shirt, and is carrying a stick. Nothing is left to chance. It is the attention to detail that makes all the difference to your peace of mind and attitude to your schooling sessions.

possible. Don't compromise any safety aspects by being too economical in your choice as you may regret it if something gives way and you part company with your horse. It isn't easy to train someone if they are on the floor because a piece of leather has snapped, or a buckle has broken.

Examine your tack as you clean it and make a note of any loose stitching that needs attention. I have seen cheekpieces and reins come undone or break while the rider is jumping, and it doesn't usually happen if the tack is in good order. You will usually see any wear and tear in the leather before it becomes dangerous, and you will be able to re-stitch or replace as necessary. Also check the metalwork to see if it is looking thin or rusty; sometimes buckles or a bit can seem to be in good condition but break without warning. It is therefore important to always buy the best quality bits because a broken bit could lead to a potential disaster.

I train a lady who used to ride her big horse in a cherry-roller mouthpiece. One day, he came round the corner to a grid and I was horrified to see bits of metal dropping from his mouth. Luckily, he was a horse who would stop immediately after a grid if we said 'good boy' so we both instinctively shrieked 'good boy George' and thankfully he pulled himself up. The metal under the rollers had snapped in two without warning as that part of the bit was covered by the rollers. Now, if I see anyone using that sort of bit I will tell them what happened, as it is the sort of thing that could lead to a tragedy. Since that time I am really only comfortable with bits if I can see the whole thing. I also feel anxious if Happy Mouth, Nathe or rubber bits start to look chewed, especially as the wire in the middle may be thin. Be warned, be careful, and only buy the highest quality bits.

Choice of saddle

The British Show Jumping Association (BSJA), show jumping's ruling body, has just introduced a new rule saying that saddles must be worn in competition, which I was quite surprised to see as I can hardly imagine anyone wanting to jump or compete without one! However, at least you know where you are with the Association, and you won't be able to economize and compete bareback, even if you wanted to.

Your choice of saddle is vital as you don't want to inhibit how you jump by using a saddle that places you in the wrong position to start with. Whatever you intend to do with your horse and however ambitious and experienced you may be, you will always need to tack up before you get on board, and so if you want to start jumping with a view to doing it better, you might have to rethink your views on saddles. You have to have a saddle and, if you choose the right one, it may enhance your position for jumping and does not necessarily have to be used exclusively for jumping.

> **Q** *Do I need a special jumping saddle before I start jumping?*
>
> **A** *Not necessarily.*

There is such a vast selection of saddles available, ranging from the synthetic-material ranges at the lower-price end of the market to specialist saddles costing a couple of thousand pounds plus.

Some of the specialist jumping saddles can have a rather exaggerated styling, which makes them unsuitable for leisure or general-purpose riding. They almost try to force you into the correct position for jumping. If they don't quite fit your contours, length of leg and size of bottom, then you will just be uncomfortable. Remember, the ideal jumping position is for all the weight to be suspended from the stirrup bars over the fence with the seat 'floating' a little, not too far forward over the front of the saddle and not bumping down on the back.

If large knee and thigh blocks aren't exactly in the right place for your particular shape, they will hamper, not help, the way you adopt this position. A decent general-purpose saddle is more than adequate to help your position and balance in the air without you being too artificially placed. Certainly it would be wise to choose one with forward-cut and padded knee panels to accommodate your knee when you are using stirrups shorter than the normal hacking length, but you don't need too prominent or angled knee rolls.

It will also help if there is a small thigh roll behind your leg to encourage the leg to sit 'in' to the flaps for comfort and stability. Again, you don't want prominent blocks in the crook of your knee in case they are not exactly in the right place for your particular anatomy.

When you try a saddle, try standing up in trot for a few strides and see if the leg is supported and comfortable enough both in front and behind (Figure 1.2). Standing trot is the only exercise I would recommend for finding your balance and feeling the best position to be in over a fence. Hold on to the martingale neck strap to start with so that you don't catch the horse in the mouth.

Try to keep your hip, knee and ankle joints 'soft' enough to absorb the motion of the horse so that you can continue this standing position for several strides. When you can do this and stay in balance without hanging on to the neck strap, then you have found the perfect position to be in over a fence. To maintain the standing-trot position you

Figure 1.2 Does your saddle support you in standing trot?

will have to be inclined forward enough – the best jumping position over a fence – or else you will bump down on the back of the saddle. If you can manage to do this comfortably for a few strides without tipping over the horse's shoulder or bumping down on the back of the seat, then you will know that the saddle is going to be acceptable for jumping.

If the knee or thigh rolls are uncomfortable and don't encourage you to stay in this sort of position, try another saddle. You must feel comfortable and supported, not contorted, and it is well worth taking the time and trouble to find the right saddle for you.

If you find a nice second-hand saddle, have a good, hopefully unbiased, saddle fitter look at it to make sure it isn't the wrong size and shape for your horse. You will soon find a horse resistant to everything if his back is being pinched. You should be able to see for yourself if anything else you acquire fits or not, but the saddle is a bit more complicated and needs an expert to check it over. Just beware the fitter who is too keen to promote the saddles he has to sell, and thinks any other brand is inferior.

Once you have your saddle sorted out, you need to choose saddle accessories that will be helpful and safe, both for you and the horse. Even with a comfortable saddle, you need the right stirrups and girth to help you on your way to better jumping.

Q *I want the stirrup leathers to last. What sort should I buy?*

A *Comfortable and safe.*

Most modern saddles have the stirrup bars well recessed and consequently there are no bulges under the thigh and so you don't want to spoil the advantages of the saddler's design by using inappropriate stirrup leathers.

Modern stirrup leathers are strong but much finer and more user-friendly than the more traditional type used in the not too distant past. They lie comfortably under the leg and shouldn't pinch like the old-fashioned rawhide or thick hunting type leathers. Some of the leathers I see in use look positively unsafe, and when the riders use the number of holes to establish whether or not they are of equal length, they may find that one stirrup has stretched and can be as much as an inch or two longer than the other. If the leather has stretched so much that the middle section is narrower and the holes are elongated into a long oval instead of the original aperture, throw them away before you have an accident. It is a false economy to use thicker stirrup leathers, purely because you think they will last longer. They may bulge under your leg and be uncomfortable. If you are not very big and don't intend to lend your tack to a taller friend, children's length leathers will be fine, and you will avoid yards of spare leather flapping on the horse's flank.

Remember that when you are jumping and your weight is in the right place, the leathers are the only thing keeping you safely in balance and position; it is, therefore, very risky to let your leathers stretch and deteriorate. Every time you clean your tack, change the leathers over so that you don't have unequal stretching because of the extra stress put on the near-side leather when you mount. Unequal or uncomfortable leathers will not help you jump better.

Q *Stirrups vary so much in price. Which should I choose?*

A *Choose for safety first, style or fashion second.*

When it comes to selecting stirrups, always opt for the safety aspect over style. I have seen some

dreadful incidents with riders hung up by the foot, which, thankfully, did not end in disaster as the horses generally stood still. But there will always be an exception to the rule.

One lady rider I train was hung up on an excitable thoroughbred who, in panic, lashed out until the stirrup leather broke. She was very lucky to have only been kicked on the leg, rather than her head. I was amazed to see her willing to get on again with the same stirrups after such a frightening experience. She seemed to think that such an occurrence was just an occupational hazard of riding and in the past it probably was. But it doesn't have to be any longer. I put a pair of my own safety stirrups on her saddle, and refused to teach her again until she got her own. There are so many ordinary mishaps involved when horses are doing anything, let alone jumping, and if the rider can do something to minimize the risks, they owe it to themselves and their families to do so.

There are several safety-stirrup designs to choose from but I prefer to see my riders using the ones that open on a hinge in an emergency (Kwik Out) or those that are reinforced on the outside edge with rubber tubing that will come off the lugs (Mountain Horse).

The Kwik Outs look like conventional steel stirrups and have very effective non-slip treads to encourage the foot to stay in the right place.

The Mountain Horse stirrup looks like a superior version of the children's safety irons, but is far more substantial and stylish. It has a special tread with grooves designed to correspond with the grooves in the Mountain Horse range of boots, making these irons extremely effective for preventing the loss of stirrups. They also give the rider options for different foot positions. Some riders prefer to have just the toe in the iron while others like to have most of the foot, up to the instep, in it. The Mountain Horse grooves allow for and support both extremes as well as the more conventional central or middle placement.

Both systems work very efficiently. Every time I have seen a rider using them come off, the outside edge has opened wide to release the foot and, so far, I haven't seen either stirrup open accidentally. The knowledge that your stirrups will release your foot in times of stress will certainly give you, and especially your trainer, a little more confidence when you are jumping

Q *Do I need a numnah?*

A *Yes.*

You really should use a numnah, if only to keep the saddle clean and stop dirt, sweat and grease building up next to the horse's skin. Numnahs are very much a question of personal taste, and they certainly can look smart as well as being practical. They may be saddle-shaped or square, cotton, sheepskin, or with spaces for gel pads or other types of inserts. You can buy embroidered ones, different colours, different sizes, the choice is endless, but don't forget that if you need to use a thick or shaped numnah to make the saddle fit better, you are probably using the wrong saddle!

When my horse is clipped right out, I use a sheepskin numnah (Stephens) shaped to fit my saddle, because I like how it looks. It is a comfort-zone buffer between the saddle and the horse, and is a substitute for his missing coat. But it is the same thickness all the way under the saddle and doesn't influence how the saddle fits. When the weather is warmer and he has a full coat, I use a cotton square numnah (Polypads) which absorbs the sweat and keeps the saddle clean underneath.

Gel pads are now very popular and can be very helpful as shock absorbers if the horse is slightly sensitive or cold backed. They can also prevent

discomfort to the horse if the rider is not too secure and bumps about a bit in the saddle.

Whichever numnah you choose, try to find one that fits the saddle as well as looking smart. It is annoying for you and uncomfortable for the horse if the numnah wrinkles up or slips back. He certainly won't jump better if he is uncomfortable, and neither will you if you are distracted by the need to adjust your tack.

Q *Should I use a jumping girth, or will my ordinary one do?*

A *A stud-guard girth is the better option.*

Girths, again, are very much a matter of choice, but I would always advise using a stud-guard girth for any jumping activity. Again, think safety first every time. If you can protect your horse, do so. It's very easy to see if your horse needs one or not. Pop one on and check the guard area. You will probably be pleasantly surprised at how far your horse tucks his feet up; high enough to leave a mark on the girth, especially when he is wearing studs (Figure 1.3).

Even when jumping without studs, the horse will still mark the girth, so it is easy to see that ordinary shoes can still mark and bruise the horse. If you can do anything to protect the horse and make his job more enjoyable, it is well worth the outlay. He won't jump so cleanly if picking his feet up high results in a pang of discomfort or pain and he will soon recognize how to avoid the discomfort by not trying as hard to pick his feet up so high. Although I would advise an all-in-one stud-guard girth if possible, there are some very effective slip-on girth guards on the market. They fit onto an existing girth to protect the vulnerable area and are obviously far more economical than a complete stud-guard girth. Do make sure they fit correctly and don't move in use because if they skew round or flap the horse can

Figure 1.3 Nicky's careful horse could easily catch herself without a stud guard.

receive some nasty rubs on the fleshy folds of skin at the inside top of the leg.

A correctly fitting stud-guard girth can make all the difference to helping your horse jump better by eliminating any abrasions your horse might receive as he tries hard to clear the fence. You too will feel better of course in the knowledge that you have done as much as you possibly can to protect your horse's vulnerable area. When you work so hard to encourage your horse to jump cleanly and accurately, you really don't want a purely physical reason to work against you (Figure 1.4).

> **Q** *If I use boots for jumping, will it make my horse careless?*
>
> **A** *No, it won't.*

If your horse has a casual attitude and doesn't seem to mind if he hits poles, you need to rethink the way you work, not to alter your horse's protection.

Your horse's legs are so precious that any protection you can use to keep him safe and sound is essential. There are many things you can do to make your horse more careful, but neglecting to use boots should never be one of them. Just remember, if your horse hits a pole hard enough so that it hurts him enough to make a difference to his performance, it will probably do some physical damage. It's very easy for a horse to go lame at the best of times and so putting him in an unnecessary situation when the risk could be avoided by the use of boots is most unwise.

You should want your horse to *want* to jump cleanly and so if your horse is careless you need to think about improving his technique by better riding. Changing the boots or not using any at all will not be effective; you need to address the reason why he is knocking poles. You will find several ideas and methods later in the book to help you achieve this.

Protective boots should be an essential part of

left **Figure 1.4** B wouldn't be so neat and tidy in front if she was constantly digging into herself.

above **Figure 1.5** Jumping 5A on the practice course: thanks to the boots, stud guard, and Jo's stickability, Leo recovered from this muddle unscathed.

your kit, and there is a vast choice of boots on the market, from very smart and expensive leather to inexpensive neoprene. They must fit well to ensure that dirt doesn't get between the boot and the horse, thus causing rubs or skin reactions, and so they should be adjustable. Velcro fastenings work very well until they become dirty, so choose double lock straps to prevent them coming undone easily. A combination of Velcro plus overstraps with a hook fastening, like that on the Clarendon range, would be a wise choice as they are less susceptible to coming undone and would be far more secure under stress. (Figure 1.5)

A lot of riders use open-fronted tendon boots in the belief that they will make their horses jump better if it hurts them when they hit a pole. However, these boots can also allow more scope for injury in the event of a serious knock and so you should try to concentrate on riding the horse well to make him jump better and not rely on an element of discomfort to make him pick his feet up.

Close-fronted tendon boots are ideal as they will give added protection to the vulnerable tendon area while still protecting the leg all round.

Weighted boots should not be used in my opinion; I think how unfair they are to the horse. All they do is give the horse a false idea of the effort required and, when the weights are removed, a horse with a naturally casual attitude to his jumping will soon relapse into that mode again. Athletes who use weights to increase their strength and performance capacity know what they are doing and why they are doing it, a horse does not!

Overreach boots can be used whenever a horse is susceptible to striking in to himself, but they need to be light and not too deep. If the cheaper rubber ones are too deep and ride up and down with each step, they are very easy to trim to the correct size, and if they don't last too well, it isn't a financial disaster.

The latest-design Neoprene overreach boots are very light when dry but, as with some material ones, can be a bit soggy and heavy when wet. Again, the rider should make sure that these, too, aren't too deep and don't move up and down rubbing the coronary area at every step. They are not as easy to trim as rubber boots and so try to choose the right size and sort to start with. Westropp Neoprene overreach boots are very effective, double fastened and not so deep that they rub.

If they are shallow, they will still protect the heel and coronary area without making the flesh sore.

One of my pupils was complaining about how keeping her horse in overreach boots was very expensive. He was always splitting them! Sometimes it's very tedious explaining the obvious. I do try very hard not to be a know-all, but common sense seems to desert normally intelligent riders when faced with a repetitive expense. Surely the boots are a lot cheaper than a damaged horse, vet bills, and time off work?

> **Q** *I don't use a martingale for flatwork; do I need one for jumping?*
>
> **A** *Yes, you certainly do.*

A horse should always wear a martingale, or more specifically a running martingale, when jumping. When correctly adjusted, they remain unobtrusive unless things start to go wrong. The rings should not be up by his ears, or down too low towards his chest. When you hold the reins in the normal position, there should be no bow in the reins, and no slack in the martingale. Not only will the martingale effectively help the steering and control, the neck strap will be a handy safety aid in an emergency. If a rider has less than perfect hands, a correctly adjusted martingale will ensure that wherever the hands are pulling from, the directional pull on the horse's bit doesn't vary, it will be consistent.

Even a top-class rider will find it is impossible to always keep the hands in a perfect position, especially when jumping. In times of stress, the hands usually go up, actively encouraging the horse's head up too, especially if he wants to be uncooperative, and then it is very difficult to re-establish an even contact quickly. It is easy for a horse to evade a rider's wishes if he sticks his nose out and to the side, and it is not easy to regain the sense of direction. In this situation the martingale will, again, help you make the steering a little more reliable.

> **Q** *My horse gets a little strong when we jump. Should I change his bit?*
>
> **A** *Only if you can't steer or steady him.*

Your bit and your legs should be your main communication with the horse. Your leg will encourage activity and impulsion and the bit should be able to contain and support all the energy your leg can generate. The bit needs to work well enough for you to be able to use your leg effectively to keep the horse working harder and stronger in his rhythm rather than faster and flatter. If your horse is usually cooperative on the flat and you find it difficult to keep control only when you are jumping, then perhaps a different bit just for jumping might be advisable.

Most horses enjoy the challenge of jumping, and

can get a bit keen and unruly in their enthusiasm. Unless you are reasonably experienced, it's very easy for you to get too keen as well, imagining that you have to approach a fence harder and faster than you need to. Then you have the additional problem of being run off with afterwards instead of remaining at a consistent pace. Whoever is causing the lack of control, it needs to be sorted out.

If you normally ride successfully on the flat in a snaffle, perhaps you should try a Dutch gag, which is also called a bubble or three-ring bit, for jumping. A very important feature of this bit is the wide variety of mouthpieces available. Whatever snaffle mouthpiece your horse is used to, you should be able to find an identical version with the extra rings and gag action. You'll probably need shorter cheekpieces so that the bit sits at the right level in the horse's mouth. If your usual cheekpieces won't adjust to be short enough, the bit will hang far too low and be worse than useless, so be prepared to buy a shorter pair of cheekpieces or have your existing ones re-stitched.

You will find that this bit will give you a very wide scope for any adjustment to its severity. The same bit, with your normal mouthpiece, can be altered from having exactly the same feel and effect as your normal snaffle by being very gradually moved up the cheekpieces to lie a little higher in the mouth, and the reins can be moved down to the middle or lower ring. I repeat, do it *gradually*. Give the bit a chance to work before making it more severe.

If you do it carefully, the horse will hardly recognize you are regaining the initiative. Just make sure you understand that with better brakes, you must use more leg. After all, that's why you wanted to change in the first place. As well as feeling safer and being able to pull up, it will make your leg more effective! You should be encouraging the horse to work better, not to do an emergency handbrake stop.

There are many other bits to try if necessary, often involving some sort of pressure on the nose but, in my experience, mostly the Dutch Gag solves the problem. So often I have suggested the change and the rider has come back with 'I've tried that already and he doesn't like it!'

Of course the horse won't approve. Why should he when he's been used to dictating the pace and steering? If a change of bit means that he has to listen to the rider's wishes instead of doing his own thing, he certainly won't like it. This is why it is so essential to change things gradually. Unless the horse has reached the stage where he is becoming dangerously headstrong, a subtle change to the position of the bit will be the best approach.

If the horse starts to argue with you when you steady him, he will usually try to throw his head about to regain the initiative. You must use your legs to push and encourage him to accept the bit and to send him into a more positive contact. It won't work immediately, but be persistent. Once he starts to be more interested in what he's doing, i.e. jumping better, he will accept that a steadier pace will make life more enjoyable for both of you. Don't forget, he has probably become keener and stronger because he likes jumping, and wants to get on with it!

> **Q** *Should I use a Flash noseband or a Grackle?*
>
> **A** *Only if you must.*

If you feel you must use either, just make sure you don't do them up too tightly. They are there to prevent the horse from opening his mouth too wide, not to force him to keep it shut.

The crank versions of nosebands can be like medieval instruments of torture in inexperienced hands, and I can never resist starting a training session by loosening the strap. After a few minutes the riders have to admit that a looser noseband has not made the horse perform differently, but I know the horse is more comfortable.

My equine dentist says she always can tell when owners have cranked their horse's jaw closed too tightly and made the lie of the bit uncomfortable, forcing the bit or teeth to score, or be actively abrasive to, the inside of the horse's cheeks.

> **Q** *Can I use training aids to help my jumping? Will I be able to use them in the ring?*
>
> **A** *The short answers are, to the first question: yes, you certainly can, and to the second question: maybe!*

There is an array of training aids to help your horse's outline and improve his method of going. Check the manufacturer's claims and decide which particular aid is going to help you and your horse. But you must ask yourself whether you can keep the horse going just as well when the aids have to be removed for competitions.

A Market Harborough martingale is an aid that is acceptable to the BSJA. It may be used for affiliated competitions as long as it is only used with a snaffle bit. It enables the rider to use the leg effectively as the slight downward pull of the check strap helps prevent the horse from leaning on the rider's hands and poking his nose out. It also has the advantage of being easily adjustable from the saddle if you need to lengthen or shorten it. Once set correctly, you cannot stress the horse or overdo the tension as the slip strap will not shorten far enough to be uncomfortable for, or unfair to, the horse.

Side reins or draw reins can have a similar effect, but these aids really need to be used *only* by experienced riders. It would be all too easy for a less-experienced rider to overdo the tension. With nothing to stop the horse's head being drawn down between its legs, the horse will eventually protest,

either by bucking or rearing. In fact it might try anything to rid itself of an unbearable tension forcing its head into an unnatural position. These reins are not allowed to be used in competitions.

The Market Harborough may not be used on ponies, although running martingales are acceptable. Standing martingales may only be attached to a plain cavesson noseband. As most unaffiliated shows are run under BSJA guidelines, these rules will generally still apply to local shows too.

The running martingale, although used so commonly, must still be considered to be an aid. Correctly positioned, it will be very effective, and will be even more so if used with reins that don't slip or get pulled through the riders' fingers. I designed a rein to combat this problem.

The Mailer Bridging Rein helps riders maintain an even contact even if the horse snatches, pulls, or leans to gain the initiative. It is a great help to the rider as it encourages, not forces, the consistent hold necessary to jump better.

The reins can also help out in an emergency because the bridge will rest on the horse's neck and does not allow the reins to slip and drop irretrievably down the horse's shoulder. Even if you let go, they will still lie there, ready to be picked up again, and of course, if you push the bridge onto the neck,

it will help you back up and into balance. (Figures 1.6a–e.) An added bonus for me is that it saves my voice: I no longer have to keep shouting, 'Keep hold'; 'Shorten your reins'; 'Pick up your contact'.

Before patenting the reins, I sent them to the BSJA to be sure they would be acceptable, not just for use at home, but also in competition. The BSJA say that as the reins do not contravene the rules, they have no objection to them being used in competition. A rider can, therefore, practise with them all the time at home and then be able to use them in the ring too.

This is the ideal situation for every rider. However helpful a training aid may be while the horse is wearing it, he recognizes immediately when it isn't employed. It is entirely possible that he will then revert, albeit gradually, to the behaviour necessitating the use of the aid in the first place. Because of all the distractions and tensions found at shows,

Figures 1.6a–e Another muddle and Jack nearly loses Charlotte but because the bridging rein has rested on Jack's neck, Charlotte hasn't lost her reins and is therefore able to use the bridge to push herself back into the safety zone.

b

a

d

c

the horse may well try to exploit the situation if a rider cannot ride in the competition arena as competently as when schooling at home.

Clothes

Over the last few years, riding clothes have reached a new level of comfort and safety.

Long gone are the days of cavalry twill 'Biggles-style' jodhpurs, scratchy polo necks and uncomfortable velvet hats with hard linings and no safety harness.

Today's clothes are comfortable, practical, wash easily and, most importantly, are safer. There are no excuses for neglecting the safety factor when riding, as even the most outlandish and colourful safety headgear, for example, is constructed to a high specification today, body protectors are improving in comfort and fit all the time and boots are designed and shaped to help the rider's comfort and position.

Q *Should I wear a hat/helmet all the time?*

A *Of course, and with no exceptions to the 'rule'.*

Occasionally there are photos in the horsy magazines (particularly in the For Sale advertisements) of riders who are not wearing hats, even very high-profile people who should know better.

However well you ride or however good you think you are, accidents can happen at any time, even in the most controlled situation, and it simply isn't worth the risk. Riding hats and helmets are light, smart, and compulsory in all competitions, so it is stupid not to use one all the time.

Don't compromise on safety; never buy a second-hand hat or helmet. You simply won't know if it is safe and in as-new condition or has already had one or two good cracks on the floor.

Q *Must I wear a hairnet?*

A *You must choose the best way to keep your hair tidy.*

Your hair must always be neat and tidy; if it is of medium length it might be easier to ensure this by securing your hair in a net. If your hair is too long for a net, pull it back into a pony tail or a bun and make sure that it doesn't flow over your shoulders.

Q *Should a body protector be worn?*

A *This is a matter of choice.*

Body protectors are not compulsory in all horse sports at the moment, but they must certainly be used in racing, eventing and Pony Club cross-country events. Unfortunately, many body protectors still make you look like the 'Michelin man' and are hot and bulky to wear, which can be very off-putting. I wear a flat-race jockey standard one which is very light and flexible, although I don't like it, but age has made me see sense at last, and it is light enough to go under a show jacket without being too restricting. It's a matter of choice in many fields of riding, but I prefer all riders I am training, young or not so young, to wear them for their own good, and all children should have them on as a matter of course (Figure 1.7). It's very unusual nowadays for me to have to mention that maybe the rider should be wearing a body protector as, like me, they have worked it out for themselves.

opposite page **Figure 1.7** A well-fitting body protector and safety stirrups give everyone a little more confidence. Emily, her parents, and her trainer are more relaxed when bold little Abbie takes a flyer over number 8C on the practice course; the last part of the combination.

Q *Long boots, or short boots plus chaps?*

A *Whichever you feel more comfortable in.*

Either will do nicely, as long as the boot has a good heel and tread to discourage the foot from slipping through the stirrup. Long boots look very smart but can be restrictive if they are rigid and stiff at the ankles and you might find that the consistent little nudges you need to make to instigate impulsion are difficult. You don't want to have your whole leg moving to keep up that consistency. Many long boots, even ones with a zip up the back for ease of fitting, now have lacing at the ankle which will give you much more flexibility to move just the ankle and foot, but if you still feel restricted, try jodhpur boots and chaps for schooling, with smarter gaiters for shows.

Q *Do I need to wear gloves?*

A *It's entirely up to you.*

The wearing of gloves is down to personal preference but remember that they do offer some protection and grip, particularly in bad weather.

Competition dress requirements differ according to the governing bodies of various societies, so make sure you check out the dress codes to see what is allowed or not. Most societies that run shows now have websites with the rules clearly set out, including what clothes are acceptable or not, and so check them out before you arrive on the showground with all the wrong kit. If you don't use a computer, the societies also produce rule books and you should be able to obtain one before becoming a member. You really don't want to be pulled up by the judges for what you are wearing when you need to be concentrating on jumping clear rounds.

When training, the only clothing stipulation I have for my pupils, apart from all the obvious safety gear, which I expect to see as a matter of course, is that I would like their shoulders to be covered. I know it's nice to be cool when the weather is hot, but if you fall off with just a vest top or string straps, your shoulders will suffer as they will invariably scrape the ground to a greater or lesser degree.

So now you know what tack and clothes you need for your horse and you to get on with the jumping. As stated, keep safety in mind and never economize on the price of a good new hat or helmet. For everything else, however, don't feel you have to spend a fortune to get everything just so. There are many bargains to be found, both second-hand and new on the various websites and in catalogues and tack shops. Just make sure that anything you buy is in good condition and is not going to let you down in the near future.

When you start to jump and then begin to progress to wanting to jump better, the more comfortable your tack and clothes are, the more you will be able to concentrate on how you are riding.

Accessories

As well as the tack and clothes there are other items that are important when jumping.

Q *Should I use studs when I'm competing on grass?*

A *Yes, of course you should.*

Studs can be a real nuisance to put in, especially if your horse's shoes are a little worn, but if you don't use them, your horse will feel insecure when jumping.

Think how you feel when running on the grass, maybe playing football or golf. Flat shoes will allow you to skid, spikes or studs will give you grip. It's just the same for your horse. The last thing he needs is to be swinging through to take off or turn and his feet slip.

If nearly everyone else in the class is using studs, you cannot afford to have your horse at a disadvantage. In addition, you will both rapidly lose confidence if you are skidding and sliding round your jumps. When you see photos of the top competitors riding over a fence, you may depend that you see the shoes sporting more than just one stud, sometimes several. Although you aren't making your living by jumping horses, there is no reason why your horse should feel any less secure than the professional jumpers.

Ask your farrier to come prepared to make stud holes in your horse's shoes. Two holes in each shoe are usually adequate. Don't forget to provide him with something to plug the holes and protect them from any debris, and remember that when you need to use studs, you are going to have to dig this plug out. PVC ear plugs are ideal for blocking the stud holes when the studs are not in use and usually come out in one piece. Cigarette filters or custom-made stud-hole fillers, even home-made plugs of cotton wool are also effective. You might like to ask the farrier for two or three nails to help dig the plugs out, but small thin screwdrivers are easier and safer to use because they have a handle. They are also bigger and easier to find if you drop one. You will need a tap to clean out the thread in the holes and a spanner to screw the studs in with. Some taps are combined with a spanner fitting in the T-handle, but your knuckles will suffer if you try to use it to screw the studs in and out. An open-ended spanner, of the right size of course, is much safer and quicker to use.

There are so many varieties of studs to choose from, and I use SupaStuds as their unique design actually cleans the thread as they are screwed in.

You may need to tap very occasionally but they go in far more easily than conventional studs. Supa-Studs make a large range of studs for different ground conditions: small and sharp for firm going, larger and blunter if the ground is soft, plus a lot of options to choose from for the in-between conditions. I tend to use a slightly smaller stud on the inside edge for safety reasons.

Whatever studs you choose, make sure that you put your horse's boots on before you put the studs in, and take the studs out before removing the boots again. If your horse is ungainly, he could easily score a stud groove down his leg. It's not a good idea to let horses stand on concrete with studs in either, as the balance of the foot can be damaged, especially if you are only using one stud at each corner. Just be sensible and guard against anything going wrong. If you drop a stud and lose it in the bedding or grass, it's annoying. If you lose a nail or screwdriver, it could, at worst, be lethal.

SupaStuds have taken this problem into consideration and designed an absolutely must-have item: an elasticated fabric wristband that contains a powerful magnet. This magnet will hold four or more studs securely while you are studding up, so that the studs are always in reach yet both hands are left free. If you do lose a stud, the magnet can be used like a metal detector to find it again. The wristband is stretchy enough to fit a bare arm or over heavy clothing.

The only effect using studs should have should be positive, even if you do skin your knuckles putting them in. The knowledge that your horse is safe with a secure footing on less-than-perfect going is very reassuring. He will jump better.

Q *Should I carry a stick?*

A *Yes, you should always carry a stick.*

A stick should not necessarily be seen as a threat, but as an extra signal or aid. Of course, if your horse is going to play up or be unresponsive, it might be needed to deliver a smack. It is, therefore, always best to have one with you rather than let the moment pass while you go and fetch one.

 Do I need spurs?

A *Spurs are a matter of choice, and you must make your own mind up whether you need them or not.*

Spurs are used to inspire an insensitive horse or as a back up for a rider's lazy leg that won't work effectively. I don't like to see horses with their sides rubbed or marked by the use of spurs, but sometimes you do need a little help to make your leg more effective. There is a fairly recent design of spur, the Impuls, which has a pair of plastic spheres that revolve at the end of the spur and roll along the horse's body without causing pain (Figure 1.8). These seem to be very effective, and much kinder if the rider is not that experienced in wearing spurs.

Every governing body has its own rules about the use of whips and spurs but the common denominator is that whips and spurs must not be misused.

Jumps

You and your horse may be well kitted out, and you might have those extra items required to keep you as safe and secure as possible, but you won't be able to improve your jumping without leaving the ground. You need jumps – plus a measuring tape.

Even the most basic grids need to be set up with

Figure 1.8 Mary is wearing the plastic-tipped spurs and her horse's sides are unblemished.

care and you need to use an accurate tape measure. I use a builder's 30 m (100 ft) tape, they cost around £7–8, and I could not work without it. If the distances aren't properly measured the object of the whole exercise can be lost. It's just as easy to put the jumps in the right place as not, so get used to using a tape and don't be so conceited as to think that you can rely on your eye or pacing the distance out. All the diagrams shown later on have the distances marked on them for a reason, i.e. to encourage you to build the grids at those distances to get the best results.

If you are working in an arena, you will be able to make little marks on the fence to help you set up your grids accurately and quickly, but you will still need to measure the distances with a tape initially in order to put the marks in the right place. If you are working in a field, the tape will not only sort out the distances required, it will enable you to build the grid in a straight line.

If you have no jumps at home, you will need to hire or borrow an arena with fences, and preferably work with a sensible instructor who will ensure that the jumps are built correctly and safely, not leaving hazardous spare cups either on the wings or on the ground, as some more casual trainers do.

> **Q** *Is it a good idea to have my own jumps?*
>
> **A** *Having your own jumps is fine as long as you don't intend to jump on your own without either a trainer or friend around to help. Owning a few poles and wings can be very helpful.*

If you intend to buy your own jumps, you will find being able to work at home such an asset. It will be so easy to set up some canter poles or a small grid, even if you are working with a friend for safety's sake (and economy) rather than your trainer, and

will enable you to do it little and often, rather than having a weekly or fortnightly training session with no practice in between.

Ten minutes or so every other day before or after your normal riding plans will not overdo things, and if you work over a smaller version of the grids you have been practising with your trainer, you should not go far wrong. If you aren't happy with the way you are going, it will be so easy to reduce the difficulty of the exercise by dropping back a stage or two, or wait until you have your next training session to get back on the straight and narrow.

You don't need to buy an expensive set of jumps before you can practise successfully at home. Three or four canter poles strategically placed can help you make a real difference to the way you produce a good show-jumping canter, and if you can add a few blocks, uprights or wings as supports, you will soon have enough to practise some of the exercises prescribed.

Plastic poles are bright, light and easy to use and need no maintenance, although they are obviously more expensive than wooden ones. If you can afford them, the Polyjump wings I use in all the grid exercises are ideal. They are easy to re-site, there is no fiddling with cups and pins to alter the height of the poles and, of course, no possibility of a careless helper leaving spare metal cups and pins lying around.

Three pairs of wings and 9 or 10 poles will be adequate for building a double bounce, a double, a combination of uprights and two jumps of the figure-of-eight grid.

Five pairs of wings and 15 poles will give you so much more scope. You will be able to build bounces, a combination with two spreads as well as an upright, the figure-of-eight grid with all four fences, plus the five-fence course to practise riding tracks.

Seven pairs of wings and 20 poles are the ideal

and you will have all the material you need to build all the grids suggested. You'll be able to start with a long 7-cross bounce grid (Figure 1.9) and progress easily to combinations and figures-of-eight, five-fence course practice, as well as the too-fast-to-stay-clean and the fan grids to help your responses and accuracy with the steering.

Whatever you use for practice, just make sure you aren't neglecting your safety. Wooden wings, wooden poles, and metal cups are perfectly adequate, and until the last few years that is all there were, so don't feel you have to have smart, modern equipment to be able to work properly. Just recognize that it is a good idea to make sure all the metal cups are accounted for and the pins are attached to them, not lying loose on the ground.

If you are in an arena, build a nice straight grid along the fence, and let the fence help your steering.

If you are out in a field and you have a wooden fence, again, try to build along it. If there is no straight fence, use your tape to measure to set the grid straight and put a few ground poles down to help guide you in and out.

If there is electric fencing or wire around the edge of your working area, stay away from it and set up across the field out of harm's way.

Working safely is the important thing and so try to build the jumps with the crosses pitched at the

Figure 1.9 Anna and Dodo are using all 7 pairs of wings and most of the poles in preparation for moving on to the fan grid (see page 85) If you have enough jumps to build this type of grid, you will find it so rewarding. If you use a variety of equipment with poles of different lengths, just make sure that the middle of the grid is in line.

right angle and height, and with the middle of the jumps all in line. *Do not* leave unused cups on the wings to save time when altering the poles, and don't use poles that are so heavy as to be immoveable when a horse rattles them. They will be hard work for your helper to move quickly and easily, and you will soon run out of goodwill if the work is too strenuous. It is not good for the horse either as you do not want to cripple him if he makes a mistake. It should of course be made clear to him that you don't like him touching poles of any description.

Never jump without a responsible person in the vicinity, it is just asking for trouble. Even a minor fall can have devastating consequences if the rider is not helped immediately, and you won't be able to jump at all if you are in hospital because you have not had the right attention quickly enough. It is bad enough having a fall when someone is there, but countless times worse if there is nobody to help you and your horse when needed. Putting safety first is not a sign of weakness, just common sense; you should simply never put yourself in a position where you may regret your decision to jump alone.

2 Novice-rider grids

First steps

> **Q** I've never jumped before, what is the best way to start?
>
> **A** Firstly, assess your standard of riding.

Before you start jumping, you should be honest about your basic standard of riding. There is no way you have to be an expert on the flat, but ask yourself the following questions. Can you canter independently and safely? Are you in charge of the speed and steering? Can you stand in your stirrups and keep your balance without hanging on by the reins? If you have answered 'yes' to them all, you are ready and well prepared to start jumping. You must start with grid work, grid work and more grid work, and *don't* try to do it without some decent help on the ground.

> **Q** What is so important about grid work? Why must I do grid work at all?
>
> **A** If you want to get the basics of jumping right, stay as secure and safe as possible and learn to not only jump but also to consistently try to jump better then, this can only be achieved with grid work.

When you've never jumped before there are series of progressive grid exercises that will help you get off the mark. If you tackle the grid exercises methodically, you should find that any errors can easily be corrected before they become bad habits. And you *will* want to get it right. Once you have started jumping, all you will want to do is jump better. However proficient you become, there is *always* more to achieve. Even if you only have a few poles and ramshackle wings, if you can cobble together a few small jumps and set them in the right place at the right distance, you will find that you will literally be able to come on in leaps and bounds. If a mistake is made or you find the next level of exercises too difficult, it is so simple to go back a stage and build your confidence up again.

> **Q** Will I be able to set up some grids at home?
>
> **A** Yes, of course, but do it very carefully.

Being careful applies to more experienced riders as well as beginners. If you are working at home with your own equipment and building the grids yourself, it will take some time to set up correctly. It always takes time, even if you are used to doing it every day, and so learning how to do it properly can initially be very hard work. You will need to be so precise with the distances you want, which will involve using a measuring tape. If the distances are not set correctly, even a well-practised horse can make the grid very uncomfortable for a complete beginner. The object of the grid is to teach you how to jump and to make you balanced and secure so that you can learn to feel the actual position and control you hope to establish by repetition.

If you don't get the distances right, even the most experienced and balanced schoolmaster will feel erratic as he progresses down the grid, and you will lose any opportunity to feel what is happening consistently underneath you. It won't help you to learn and you will become more anxious rather than more confident as your horse lengthens or shortens instead of staying in the same rhythm.

Grid-work distances and related distances

Course builders at shows normally work using fairly conventional distances and this table will help you recognize how important it will be to set your grid up accurately. You certainly don't want the course builder to catch you out just for the lack of a tape measure to establish the distances to practise with!

Related distances are the distances a course builder sets between jumps, inside element to inside element. Usually using a tape for accuracy, he sets them to encourage the horse to take a conventional number of strides: *true* strides. You can see from the table of distances below that the course builder has scope to vary the distances according to the prevailing conditions at a show. Generally the longer limits of the suggested distances are used in outside arenas, the slightly shorter distances at indoor shows.

When you walk the course you must remember to take into consideration the variables, other than the way you ride, which will affect the length of the horse's stride. A horse going downhill, even if the slope is very slight, will tend to take a longer stride, so all the distances may be increased from the 'true' distance to allow for this. The converse applies when a horse is going uphill. Heavy going will shorten a horse's stride; ideal going will lengthen a

horse's stride. Going towards the exit may lengthen the stride and travelling away from the collecting ring may shorten the stride.

Just do your best and try to ride as consistently as you do in practice; you have worked so hard to establish this consistency.

Once you get beyond six or seven strides, the distance is getting long enough to not really be related any more. There would still be an optimum number of conventional strides but there would be more scope to shorten or lengthen the stride if your horse finds the consistency of the conventional length difficult to maintain over a longer distance.

Bounce or normal-length stride = 3.65 m (12 ft /4 yd)

One-stride related distance = 7.3–7.6 m (24–25 ft/8–8½ yd)

Two-stride related distance = 10–10.9 m (33–36 ft/11–12 yd)

Three-stride related distance = 13.7–14.6 m (45–48 ft/15–16 yd)

Four-stride related distance = 18.2 m (60 ft/ 20 yd)

Five-stride related distance = 21.9 m (72 ft/24 yd)

Most riders learn to pace out their distances to the yard, and it is certainly easier to remember than dealing with fractions of metres, but for the grid work, the tape is a must!

If you work in a field rather than by a fence or in an arena, you need to ensure that the grid fences are all in line and not crooked. When you progress further and want to set the grid fences on angles instead of straight lines, it takes great care to put them in the right place to get the maximum benefit from the exercises. To do your grid work properly, and if things are going smoothly, the poles will need to be altered nearly every time, or at least every three or four turns and so you won't be able to manage on your own. Once you have done an exercise well on one rein, you will need to turn the grid round which may involve a fair bit of moving, and you will need to keep changing the direction back and forth. You simply won't be able to keep up a flow if you have to get off to alter things and so realistically you need someone on the ground to deal with the poles while you concentrate on riding the horse.

Preparation for novice-rider grid work

> **Q** *How many jumps do I need?*
>
> **A** *An ideal novice-rider grid can be built with seven fences.*

Obviously you can build fewer fences but any number under three will not be very productive as it won't give you time to feel what you should be feeling; you will finish the grid before you have a chance to establish the rhythm and balance you hope to acquire. I would start with the wings in place and a line of seven poles on the ground set at the 3.65 m (12 ft) canter distance, and build up from there. When you consider all the implications of setting up even moderately simple grids, you must wonder if it is worth the effort. Be assured that *it is*.

There is no other system that is more successful for starting off a complete beginner, and this methodical and logical approach to jumping should ensure that the novice rider doesn't lose any confidence. Although the rate of progression is necessarily slow, it will be completely reliable as long as you do the right exercises in the right order. After tackling a well-built and carefully placed set of fences, you should be able to judge how well you are doing by recognizing whether what you feel when riding through the grid is right or not. Obviously, the more jumping efforts you make, i.e.

the more times you leave the gound, each time you do the grid, the quicker you will learn. Not only will it be easier to acquire a secure jumping position but a long grid will also teach you to keep going actively, to keep up the impulsion level, and to practise your steering too.

> **Q** *How many times should I go down the grid?*
>
> **A** *As many times as it takes until the work feels right.*

Do not even consider moving on to something more demanding until the work is correct. If you feel out of balance and insecure, you need an experienced person to either make a recommendation about changing your position slightly or to alter the grid subtly to make it easier for the horse to operate smoothly. But these things *do* need to be done by someone who has an understanding of the mechanics of the grid work, and the patience to keep altering things to make it easier for you. Then their instructions to: 'come again, but with more leg' or 'come again and look up' or 'come again with a bit more weight in the stirrups' or 'come again but a bit steadier' or 'come again and try for the middle this time' or 'come again and don't cut the corner' or 'come again and don't collapse at the end', will have some effect. It should always be 'come again' because there is no other way but repetition to feel and learn and develop the balance, impulsion and position that the grid will give you.

> **Q** *Are there any short cuts?*
>
> **A** *No, not if you want to learn, progress and, most importantly, stay as safe as possible.*

Three conditions will help to determine how rapidly you manage to develop your skills.

1. A nice cooperative and reasonably experienced horse.

A horse that you know and have worked with on the flat is ideal, but don't be surprised if he is surprised when you start your new adventure! He will associate you with hacking, flat work and dressage, so this will be a little new for him too. Once he realizes that it is *you* who is going to be the jumping rider, he will be fine, but you will need to have a positive attitude yourself if he is used to being jumped only by his usual jumping rider.

2. An experienced and sympathetic trainer.

A good trainer should be understanding but not too easy going, but neither should they be too tough! Riders who are new to jumping should be encouraged, not bullied, in order to be able to progress and improve steadily.

I learned a lot about the sensible rate of progress by watching other trainers and their clients. Before moving to my current yard and concentrating purely on training, I had a larger establishment with five jumping arenas, which were hired by riders to use with their own trainers. It was very interesting to watch other people's methods and I was sometimes surprised by trainers' ideas about rates of progress, particularly for novice riders. I did feel that some of the riders were very poorly treated by their experts, at both extremes.

One lady came with the same trainer for years, and never seemed to be able to do any better than when she started. The trainer was so nice and encouraging with lots of pats and congratulatory comments, but the rider was never pushed to do better. She needed a bit of a shove to move on and improve.

At the other end of the scale, some trainers would be far too ambitious for their rider's actual ability. These sessions often ended in tears, resulting in a loss of confidence as the riders were overfaced.

The ideal sessions seemed to be the ones that ended with all three participants having made a bit of progress and all looking happy, and it's an attitude I have been mindful of ever since. If there is any doubt in a trainer's mind about the rider's ability and willingness to be pushed a bit further, it should be left until another day. There is always another day. If, on the other hand, a trainer is sure that an encouraging nudge will make everyone happier then they should go for it!

You should never make a request of a novice rider without being 99 per cent certain that *you* know the outcome. Of course, even the nicest horses can be unpredictable and things sometimes go wrong, but they should never go so wrong that they can't be put right by a little extra practice at a lower level on the grid. The mutual trust will then be maintained, especially when things go right again.

Riders will not trust a trainer who is constantly on the edge of overfacing them, and any reservations about the advice given may be disastrous. At the very least, they will not look forward to the training, and they may feel like giving up instead of wanting to improve and enjoy themselves.

3. A safe environment and user-friendly equipment.

Ideally, the novice rider should start jumping in an enclosed arena. It is important to feel safe and secure with positive boundaries and, if things don't go quite according to plan, the horse will not be able to shoot off over the horizon. Even novice jumpers are far more confident about riding their horses forward if there is a secure fence at each end of the grid.

As you can see in all the grid photos, I use plastic wings and poles from Polyjumps. They are far safer than wooden equipment if horse and rider have a misunderstanding and the safety factor encourages me to be a little bolder with that which I ask of the rider. The poles will still rattle if they are knocked, but it is unlikely that the horse will be hurt if he hits one hard. Each rider I train needs a different grid to help them jump better and these jumps are light and easy enough to move around quickly to meet their requirements. Sometimes it is very helpful to the horse and rider to come round again without a rest, and it is much easier to change poles quickly when you don't have to fiddle about with cups. Of course they are not essential and they are more expensive than wooden wings and poles, but if you can afford to kit yourself out with just a few plastic poles and blocks or wings, you will find them infinitely easier to use.

Obviously it might be difficult to attain the three ideal situations simultaneously, but do your best. Even if you own your own horse, he might not be the best horse to start jumping on, so don't be afraid to look round for a well-behaved riding-school horse, for example, who knows his job. However much you would like to be independent, a riding school might well fulfil the other two conditions of an expert instructor and an arena to keep your boundaries safe. If it is difficult to achieve all the best circumstances advised, but *do not* compromise with safety.

On no account ride a horse known to be awkward and difficult simply because it may be the only one available. Leave well alone; if you have a fall because of a horse's difficult character, all you will learn is that it hurts, and you won't be too keen to repeat the experience.

Q *My horse has never jumped before, will it matter?*

A *Yes, it will matter a great deal.*

You must try to start jumping on a horse who is well behaved, experienced, knows what he's doing and is willing and cooperative. Starting on a horse who is also a novice will present you with the additional problem of having to help the horse when you don't know what you are doing. This would be a waste of time and effort and you would both end up confused and frustrated.

Q *I can't seem to find a good trainer locally. What should I do?*

A *Seek help from someone you trust.*

If a good trainer is not available, make sure that you take advice only from a calm and unflappable friend or acquaintance whose jumping ability you admire. It is not easy to find a trainer who is available, ticks all the boxes and with whom you feel at ease.

Some trainers, although very good, do not want to, or cannot, cope with complete beginners, and only want to step in with training when the rider is competent at jumping say 1.05 m (3 ft 6 in) plus. Even if their training ability is very good at that level, they lack the patience to go slowly and methodically through the early stages, which will give the beginner a good foundation on which to build their training, rather than pinpointing specific areas to work on. That will come later.

The person you choose to help you must have a strong regard for the safety of their beginner jumpers. A reliable and practical friend with plenty of common sense would be ideal as they should have your best interests in mind. A friend might not have professional training qualifications but they will sympathize with your inexperience and try hard to keep you safe rather than allowing you to fall off. Also, I hope that the grid exercises recommended are so crystal clear that a sensible helper will be able to see what is required and have the confidence to suggest ways of improving the exercises.

At this early stage it is not rocket science! It will

be obvious if the rider is not using enough leg as the horse will not go smoothly; it is easy to see if the rider is looking down or waving their hands about instead of having a couple of fingers tucked safely into the neck strap, and if the rider can't organize their weight to hang securely from the stirrup bars, they will be unsteady and an ordinary observer should be able to see if the stirrups may be a little too long.

Asti and Stephanie

> **Q** *Stephanie is ready for her first lesson; has she achieved the three conditions?*
>
> **A** *Yes.*

Stephanie's own horse is a complete novice with no jumping experience and so she has elected to have her first lesson on her daughter's horse Asti. Asti jumps competitively with daughter Siobhan (Figure 2.1); he is well practised in grid work and so is an ideal choice for a complete beginner. It really is an asset to know the horse that you are riding, so before you start jumping try to be conversant or familiar with the horse on the flat. You need to be relaxed and confident before you leave the ground, otherwise any tension will spoil the way you ride and you will struggle to get the most out of your training. As Stephanie keeps Asti fit during the week, she knows him pretty well.

Stephanie and Asti are starting off with my help in a secure environment, and she will do her early work in a fenced arena where she can concentrate on riding forwards and have no worries about pulling up safely after a grid exercise.

Even at this very early stage it isn't too soon to start practising what you will need to be doing in the future when you want to tackle more progressive grids and then different jumps and courses. As long as you can canter comfortably with your

Figure 2.1 Asti working with Stephanie's daughter Siobhan.

weight in the stirrups and a slightly elevated seat, the first exercise should just feel as simple as an exaggerated canter.

After watching Steph try to canter with a floating seat, you can see her stirrups are very slightly on the long side; her toe is seeking the stirrup (Figure 2.2). Once they are taken up a hole she mustn't let the shorter length make her stand taller in the stirrup but rather have a bit more 'softness' through her knee and ankle. I want her to think 'down' into the stirrup so that her weight is hanging off the stirrup bars rather than bearing heavily on the back of the saddle. Her shock-absorber joints must be flexible and elastic.

As soon as she adjusts to this and feels comfortable, she is ready to come down a long line of 7 poles on the ground. Steph must not be put off by the length of the grid as the poles are set very precisely at the 3.65 m (12 ft) distance, a bounce, so

that each effort from Asti should be more or less identical. The distance between the obstacles must be carefully set to encourage the horse to canter smoothly down the grid. Steph has been told to expect an exaggerated canter feeling but she doesn't want any surprises because the distances are wrong.

If a horse has to shorten or lengthen his bounce stride to get a jump right, it won't be very comfortable for a complete beginner. Check the distances chart and make sure you use that measuring tape to set the distances exactly. Any variation or casual pacing will do more harm than good, even if you are only a few inches out at each distance.

Even at such an early stage, when riding her very first grid, Steph is encouraged to try to look up to *feel* what is happening underneath her, rather than looking down to *see* what is happening. It's never too soon to establish good habits, and keeping your head up is one of the best.

Figure 2.2 The stirrups are a little too long.

You must look where you want to go. Don't just cast your eyes round the corner with your head square to his ears. It's not dressage! Physically turn your head; it is your horse's early warning system. If Steph turns her head to look round the corner at the line of poles before she gets to it, Asti will pick up on her intentions a fraction sooner and be much surer to understand where he's meant to be going.

Steph is asked to approach the grid coming round the corner in trot, and then ask for canter when she is square to the first pole. If he doesn't meet it perfectly so that it comes in the middle of his stride, he is experienced enough to make any adjustment and carry on through smoothly as long as Steph keeps pushing. The trot approach is sensible as Steph will have so much to think about, and she doesn't want to be travelling too fast to be able to steer accurately.

If Steph doesn't achieve canter in time it won't matter; Asti will just keep trotting down the line. A ground pole is not usually quite enough to make him feel the need to elevate and then carry on in canter. She can just come round again and have another go. Once she gets the hang of it, her steering becomes more natural, her canter aids are a little more positive and are given a little earlier, and Asti pops over the canter poles with hardly a change in his way of going. However obedient he is, it does make Steph appreciate that she must keep up some consistent friendly nudges from her heels to make it easy for him to maintain his rhythm and length of stride. When she doesn't do quite enough, the last two or three poles are a bit of a stretch for Asti, and even a complete beginner like Steph will feel it. Although very well behaved and experienced, he isn't a complete pushover, so Steph must actually ride him; she can't afford to be just a passenger. With all her weight dropping down into the stirrups, her bottom floating slightly off the saddle and with a couple of fingers tucked in the martin-gale neck strap to stay secure, Steph tries to nudge Asti over each canter pole.

Once they are looking a confident partnership down a long line of poles, the grid is altered in six steps as shown in Diagram 1 (page 32). These grid variations can also be used for the novice horse (see Chapter 3).

The grid is built up into a series of very small crosses (Step 1). This will help Steph steer down the middle and just take a little more initiative in the exercise. Steph is still encouraged to approach round the corner in trot to make sure she is steady enough and in a position to push on to the grid. Once again, it does not matter if Asti goes into canter before the grid, or if he stays in trot. The cross is just enough to encourage him to jump and once he pops in over the first one, he should land in canter and with Steph's encouragement he will then canter on through.

For a newcomer to jumping, everything happens very quickly, so going too fast is definitely not encouraged. Trotting in is sensible as it would be far too easy for an onward-bound horse to zip round the corner in canter and miss the grid entirely, purely because the rider is inexperienced. Asti is very well behaved, but sometimes even the best-mannered horses get a bit keen when jumping, especially with a novice rider. Even if the crosses are very small they will still encourage Steph to ride down the middle of the grid. It's never too early to start learning to ride to the middle of the fences (Figure 2.3), and with a long grid you will soon discover if you can ride a straight line or not.

Steph practised this grid several times and was really enjoying herself; Asti appeared to be having fun too. This was genuinely a first lesson and so, although I was ready at any stage to call a halt if necessary, because everything was going so well there was no reason at all not to take the lesson a little further.

Diagram 1 Grid for novice riders and novice horses

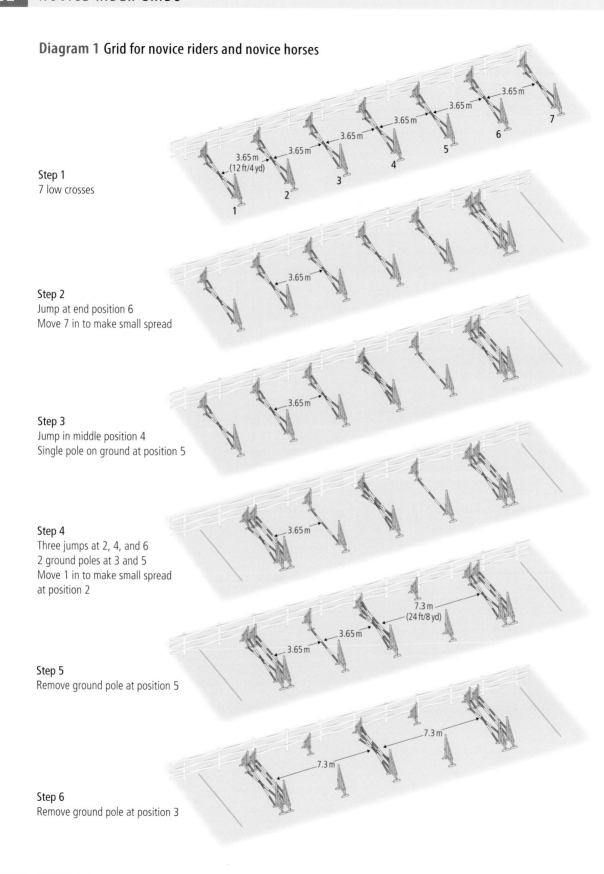

Step 1
7 low crosses

Step 2
Jump at end position 6
Move 7 in to make small spread

Step 3
Jump in middle position 4
Single pole on ground at position 5

Step 4
Three jumps at 2, 4, and 6
2 ground poles at 3 and 5
Move 1 in to make small spread
at position 2

Step 5
Remove ground pole at position 5

Step 6
Remove ground pole at position 3

When you use 7 crosses it is very easy to change the grid so gradually that the horse and rider hardly realize you have done it. I like to build up the end (position 7) jump first and probably the next step would be to move the end jump in behind position 6 and make a very small parallel behind the cross (Step 2 and Figure 2.4).

Depending on how well a rider is balanced, I would probably make the number 5 cross even lower, still leaving a cross to encourage them to aim for the middle. With the cross lower, the horse will be encouraged to keep going in his rhythm and won't need to make such a springy jump at the last which might shift the novice rider.

Steph is going so well that I can alter the grid very slightly after each exercise. As long as she keeps riding in the same way, she makes rapid progress. If we find an exercise that is not ridden so well, we just repeat it until everyone is happy.

If you are trying this at home, when you are going smoothly and you are remaining secure over the last fence, the next step is to make number 4 into a small upright but with a cross in front of it on the take-off side (Step 3). Again I would make the number 3 cross lower and possibly the number 5 cross into a single pole on the ground. I don't want the horse's action to be too exaggerated over number 4 to shift you out of position. The single pole on the ground in the 5 position will keep the horse coming smoothly and regulate his speed and rhythm so you can stay balanced. Even with a very basic small grid it is easy to produce a bigger jump from the horse by the distance and size of the crosses and you don't want an experienced horse to be too sharp and extravagant off the ground and unbalance you. The poles left on the ground or as very small crosses encourage the horse to stay in a smooth rhythm consistently, neither rushing nor backing-off the actual jumps.

When you are happy with that grid, move on to

top **Figure 2.3** It is never too early to practise riding straight down the middle.

below **Figure 2.4** Asti is giving Steph a grand feel of jumping but Steph must look up more and start to work on this tendency to lean in slightly and drop the inside shoulder; the shoulders should be level. It might seem that I am nit-picking a little, criticizing at this very early stage, but it's much better to develop good habits from the start rather than let the bad ones become established.

Step 4. Make numbers 1 and 2 into a jump at number 2 position. If you are going well and feel secure and confident, make this jump a cross pole on the first pair of wings, with horizontal poles behind making a small spread jump going in, just like the last jump on the grid. If you are still slightly anxious or inconsistent with your approach and a little unsteady through the grid, carry on with the original grid a few more times, then make the first jump in with a cross on the number 2 wings as well as the horizontal poles, minimizing any spread. We don't need the horse to enjoy himself too much and take too big a leap in! If everything is still going smoothly at this stage, make number 3 just a pole on the ground, so effectively there are three jumps with two ground poles midway between them.

I would then hope to remove the ground poles one at a time and I would remove number 5 first (Step 5). If you can carry on through the grid two or three times successfully, keeping up the necessary impulsion without the pole to help your horse, then remove the ground pole at number 3 position (Step 6). Now, be it ever so small, we have the novice rider jumping through a combination which is a huge achievement for a first timer (Figure 2.5).

Don't worry if you have to stop before reaching this point, everyone has their own rate of progress, and there is no need to feel pressurized or overfaced. If you have a wobble at any stage, just go back a step and repeat the previous grid a few more times until you feel relaxed about moving on again; or you could just rest on your laurels and leave moving on until next time. You shouldn't have a rigid plan or set yourself a timescale as you will inevitably end up disappointed. Let your trainer/helper inject some common sense into the proceedings and take notice if they think you have done enough for one day (Figure 2.6).

Figure 2.5 Steph and Asti making a lovely job of this small combination.

Because Steph was so keen to try a 'real' jump, and I could see no reason why she shouldn't, we asked Asti to just pop over a small jump in the arena (Figures 2.7a and b).

Steph was warned in advance to be positive, to remember all she had learned from the grid work, to ride the same way even though the jump is different and, above all, to *enjoy* herself. It must be emphasized that when you leave the grid to try a jump you think might be more demanding, it is absolutely vital to try very hard to keep riding *in exactly the same way*.

right **Figure 2.6** Steph has made real progress in her first session and is looking very confident. It is time to take stock and think about calling it a day.

Figures 2.7a and **b** With no crosses to help Steph with her steering, she makes a very good approach to the middle of the jump and, although her balance wobbles slightly as Asti tries to cut in, she certainly looks as if she is enjoying it.

a

b

Progression

Once that feeling and position is established over even the tiniest grid, you won't need to change the way you ride when the jumps get bigger. Because you should be trying hard to get in the habit of producing maximum impulsion and power from the very beginning, you shouldn't have to try harder when the jumps are more imposing, as you should already be doing enough.

The only difference you should find when jumping a bigger fence is that you will be in the air longer, therefore you must hold or hover your position over the fence a split second longer to allow your horse to keep his back feet in the air long enough to clear it.

The position shouldn't change from that you adopt when riding over a small grid, but if you get your timing wrong and anticipate your horse's descent, you will shift your weight too early and this will make him rattle the pole behind.

Your trainer/helper must be very careful to judge your progress and not try anything too demanding too soon. It's very easy to upset the confidence of a complete beginner and the object of the exercise is to have fun and learn. Even as a complete novice to jumping you should already be developing the rudiments of producing impulsion, looking up, steering down the middle and not tipping too far forward too soon.

When you see photos of the top showjumpers, they are nearly always showing the rider at the top of the jump where they appear to be leaning forwards as they jump. You might, therefore, feel that you need to arrange yourself into this forward position before take-off instead of waiting for the horse to come up underneath you. Even at this very early stage, try to recognize how much you need to allow yourself to feel what is happening rather than trying to adopt what you perceive to be the 'jumping position' too early before your take-off point. Try very hard to wait for the horse's neck to come up to meet your chest, rather than you making the first move and bobbing down to meet him. Think of following the horse instead of being in advance of him in your enthusiasm to do well.

Trainers have to be so careful not to overface their riders and with the correct pairing of the right horse with a novice rider, the rider can learn so quickly about how much they need to do with their legs, how to steer, and how to develop their balance. If the novice grid is built carefully and the rider is not hurried by changing the grid exercises too quickly, they will finish the session feeling elated with a real sense of achievement, not only for having actually jumped, but also for having jumped better.

There isn't a manual and set rules for a trainer because each combination of rider and horse is different, but if you do the right grids using the correct methods with patience, you will, without fail, get your riders and horses jumping better. The only uncertain element in the equation is the amount of time and number of sessions it will take. The rider must be patient, willing to work hard, and not look for a quick fix.

Although there are exceptions, 95 per cent of riders, and not just novices, will need very similar advice or reminders to help them improve at every level, and I usually find that I give the same instructions and guidance at each training session, from novice to advanced level. Certainly with more experienced riders the advice is usually, although not always, more subtle! But even the very best riders need help on the ground to keep them maintaining their level of excellence.

Instructions

'**Leg on!**' is the priority instruction. Without a consistent and encouraging leg, you won't have impulsion, and without impulsion your jumping will be erratic at best and non-existent at worst.

'**Keep hold**': maintain as consistent a contact on the reins and with your horse's mouth as possible all the way through the grid, even with some fingers slipped through your neck strap for security. Using the neck strap in this way will actually help your hands to stay in the best position and so you should not feel it is a childish thing to do. Anything which helps you ride the grid better is a bonus. The more consistent your contact is, the more support you will be able to give your horse to encourage him to do well. However much leg you use, if you don't contain the energy in front, all that leg effort will be wasted. You have to have a partnership with your horse if you want to jump better, and if he can rely on you consistently gathering his energy and impulsion, he will find the job much easier, not only when you are popping over a small grid but also as you become more ambitious with your jumping later on.

It is vital that you '**look up**'. When riders start looking down at the poles to see what they are doing instead of where they are going, they will tip forward, give the reins away and lose the contact and then whatever impulsion your legs have generated will just dissipate.

I find that the instruction '**chin up**' works wonders for the whole body position. Without being too technical, a rider who slightly exaggerates lifting the chin in the air will immediately be better balanced. They will be straighter and their shoulders more level. The weight will drop more into the stirrups, the ankle, knee and hip joints will be more giving and flexible, and from this position a rider would have to be a contortionist to be able to lean too far forward over the horse's neck. It is such a simple thing to try, and produces such a good result for both rider and horse. It is a very good habit for more advanced riders to form too, especially if they are having front-leg knockdowns. The earlier this particular principle for better jumping is established, the easier jumping will be both in the early and advanced stages.

'**More outside rein**' is an instruction riders will often hear. The use of the outside rein gives more control over the steering, the impulsion and the horse's cooperation and obedience. It will prevent him zooming around, cutting corners and, if you use the right amount of inside leg into your outside rein, you will come off your turns with more power to cope with the next line of fences.

You will soon discover what works and the degree of strength of leg to hand (or contact) required to get the best feel; it is so easy to practise initially on a straight grid, and then more advanced grids set on a figure-of-eight course when you are ready. Never forget, if it feels OK, it probably is.

3 Novice-horse grids

All the grids and the changes suggested in the Novice-rider grids chapter are perfect for teaching the novice horse how to jump.

Actually, 'teach' is the wrong word to use. When starting a completely novice horse the attitude required is that of a determination to **allow the horse to learn**, rather than trying to force the exercises and help or organize him too much.

Think about giving the horse a set of circumstances like the ground poles and then riding him forwards and over them. Let him sort it out. You mustn't try to help him in any way except to ask and, if necessary, insist that he moves forward from your leg. Don't give him a choice; if he becomes stubborn nag him with your legs until he gives in. They are only poles on the ground and it should not be a major issue. You want him to discover that if he goes forwards the poles are easy and fun, not hazards set there to catch him out. He might think it a little unusual to step over things when you are riding him, but he will have been managing his feet all his life. Unless he has led a very sheltered existence he will have stepped over lots of things quite naturally. It is always a good idea before you start a complete novice to leave a few old poles in the field, surrounding his feed bucket or water, or maybe just in the gateway, so that he has to step over a pole to get where he wants to go. The novice horse will soon become blasé and then bold and confident about them.

If a horse hasn't been used to wearing boots, a martingale, or any of the other equipment suggested to keep him as safe and protected as possible, make sure you use the kit a few times before you ask him to jump. He doesn't need too many strange things to deal with at once.

Again, the seven poles are ideal but you might feel with your novice horse that you would prefer to start with just one pole, then two, then three and so on. Be bold yourself. You might be pleasantly surprised if you start with a long grid and are prepared to nag strongly with your leg. Your horse may be uncertain to start with, but the further you encourage him down the grid, the more he will learn. It is always nice to see the complete novice gain confidence and be much bolder over the last couple of poles, positively pleased with himself for being so brave.

A fenced arena is the best place to start, and you must try to position your grid right beside the fence if possible, you will then only need to worry about the horse running out on one side. Hopefully it won't happen, but it is far better to be prepared, and the fence will also make it easier for you to ensure that the grid is in a straight line.

With experienced horses and riders, I will often set the grid 0.6 m (2 ft) or so away from the fence, which makes the whole thing far more difficult. I am not playing a trick on them or trying to make it unfair, it is just to make sure they are looking where they are going instead of simply letting their horses follow the fence line or track round the corner and along the approach. It means the rider's steering ability has to be a little more independent; it also makes the rider look far enough ahead to where they are meant to be going in order to straighten up to the middle of the grid without bulging out on the turn. However, that particular exercise will only need to be set in the future.

The novice horse doesn't need a long run up for his approach. You will only be walking to start with and when you work in trot or canter, if the approach is a little on the short side so much the better because you will both have far less time to get it wrong. So many riders think that the more room they give themselves on the approach, the more chance the horse has of doing the grid well but, in my experience, that extra time and room gives the rider far more time to fiddle with the stride and rhythm and lose the impulsion necessary to do a good job. If you ride a decent corner keeping the horse working in to a supportive outside rein, the inside hind leg comes through strongly and you should come off the turn with lots of impulsion. It seems only logical to recognize that if the grid is only four or five strides off the turn, it is easier to maintain that impulsion all the way to the first obstacle, rather than having to keep up the momentum for eight or ten strides.

If you cannot build the grid against a fence, it is essential to make sure the grid is in a straight line. Use a builder's 30 m (100 ft) tape to set up your jumps. If you are building the grid up on your own, peg the end of the tape to the ground so that it cannot move and then unroll it where you want the grid to be. Using a tape religiously will not only make sure that your jumps are in a straight line, but your measurements will also be accurate to the inch. It is also advisable to measure the distance on both sides of the grid. This is not being overtly fussy; it is quite amazing to discover how badly your eye can lead you astray and one side of the grid may not accurately match the distance of the wings on the other side! If you are working in a field without a fence line, place some guiding poles at the beginning and end of the grid to help both you and your horse with the approach and exit.

If you have plenty of equipment, use guide poles on either side of the grid going in and coming out. If you don't have many spare poles, place the approach guideline on the outside to prevent the horse bulging out or overshooting the approach. Another pole at the exit on the inside will help the rider prevent the horse from leaning in and cutting across after the grid is completed. Don't forget to alter the poles to the opposite side when you do the grid in the other direction.

There is just one more point to consider. If your poles are not uniform and are different lengths, make sure that they are set so that the horse actually goes over the middle of the poles in a straight line, even if it means having some of the wing pairs set either a little in or out. When you build the grid into crosses, you won't want your horse going over the crosses in slalom fashion because the middle of the crosses is not in line. Remember, it is the centre of the jump that the horse needs to negotiate.

Attention to this sort of detail will help to prevent your horse developing bad habits, even at this very early stage, and will help you both to get the most out of the work.

Novice-horse grid 1

Seven poles set at the canter distance, i.e. 3.65 m (12 ft) would be the ideal starting point. Don't forget that with the novice horse the canter-pole distance will give you three walk strides, two trot strides and one canter stride, but always walk and then trot over the poles before you think of trying to canter. If you find that you need to have the poles a shorter or longer distance apart in walk and trot to adjust to your horse's natural stride, you must then alter them so that the canter stride will be correct. It is easy to judge from walk and trot if your horse has a conventional stride or is short- or long-striding.

In the early sessions you can shorten or lengthen the distance between the poles and small crosses to accommodate the horse's stride. Only when he is tackling them confidently in canter should you gradually move them out or shift them in to the conventional 3.65 m (12 ft) distance by inches. This 'conventional distance' rule is not written in tablets of stone but you must realize that this is the distance course builders will base their doubles, combinations and measured related distances on when they build at shows. They normally work setting fairly conventional distances and the table on page 25 will help you recognize how important it will be to set your grid up accurately, and so do make sure you use your tape.

When you have your distances measured accurately, pace them out over and over again on your own two feet until you could do it in your sleep. When you are walking a course, you need to know exactly how the course builder has set his distances.

The completely novice horse needs to feel relaxed and confident at this stage. Once you are satisfied that he is happy in walk and trot, you can ask him to canter. Remember that it is only when he is going well in canter that you should start to fiddle with distances if necessary. (See Chapter 12, The value of canter poles.) Most horses are fairly happy with the 3.65 m (12 ft) canter stride but if not you need to work hard to ensure they can do it consistently. If you can get your horse to produce this canter stride it is one less thing to worry about when you start to jump courses. When you progress you don't want him to get in a pickle at double or treble combinations purely because he is making up too much ground and getting too close to the second element

or he is not working hard enough to make up enough ground to make the take-off point easily.

Don't be in too much of a hurry to change the length of your horse's stride if he is comfortable with it, however, just keep using more leg to persuade him to lengthen his stride if necessary or simply avoid being too pushy and forward yourself if he already prefers to canter at 3.96 m (13 ft). Nonetheless, if you allow a big horse to bowl along and make up too much ground for too long without trying to adjust and regulate his length of stride in the very early stages, he is going to get in more of a muddle than the shorter-striding horse (Figure 3.1). You must try hard to produce an 'up' canter over the poles rather than a long one. It is easier to encourage the shorter stride to lengthen than it is to gather up the sprawling long stride into a neater and shorter outline.

When your horse is happy over the canter poles, change the grid into small cross poles; changing one for each turn down the grid, starting with the last jump and moving consecutively backwards to the first. This will be his very first jump, so just make sure *you* are very positive. Set the cross at a very low height, it is a perfect exercise to encourage a novice horse to learn how to manage his legs, and work out for himself that the more he is obedient to the leg and goes forward, the easier he will find the exercise. Even if he is anxious when he sees that the grid has changed and walks or trots over the poles to start with, his confidence will grow and he will become more willing if you give him no opportunity to do anything else. Concentrate on encouraging him to go forward down the line and to sort his own legs out. The more you can ride him from your leg into a supportive and consistent contact, the more willing he will become. At this distance and this height, it will be a very straightforward exercise for him if he listens to your leg and allows it to encourage his impulsion.

If he trots through and stays in trot over the cross, don't try to force him to canter and jump. As stated, you really want him to learn for himself without you doing anything but encouraging him forward from your leg into a supporting contact. As you build more crosses, he should find it easier to canter but, again, don't force him. As long as you produce plenty of energy, let him work it out for himself. Normally the horse will do a good job and jump out over the last cross in the line, but if he persists in trotting higher and higher, just make the last cross higher by raising the sides and creating a sharper 'X' shape (Figure 3.2).

Most horses enjoy jumping and although your novice might be a bit suspicious initially, he should not have had any bad experiences to put him off. If

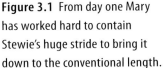

Figure 3.1 From day one Mary has worked hard to contain Stewie's huge stride to bring it down to the conventional length.

Figure 3.2 A sharper 'X' shape in the cross will almost certainly encourage the horse to jump instead of staying in trot.

a horse *has* had a bad time and needs to go back to the beginning and be treated like a complete novice again, these exercises should help his confidence.

Do remember that the only feedback you will get from the novice horse is from your observation. Novice riders can tell you exactly how they are feeling if they are getting tired or worried and it is easy to discuss with them the wisdom of whether or not to do a little more. Novice horses can only show you whether they have done enough by their demeanour and willingness – or lack of it – to keep going, and you must make sure you are ready to listen to them.

If a horse is happy, confident and well ridden, it is possible to start a novice's first session with the ground poles and finish it with him jumping a small combination of three tiny jumps in a row, but every horse has his own rate of progress. Once a horse realizes what fun it can be when he goes forward, he will find the grids easy and you must call a halt before he gets over-confident and over-ambitious; such arrogance could lead to him making a mistake. Make sure you guard against him starting to rush: don't be afraid to **say 'steady'** and **think 'wait'**. You won't put the stoppers on him if you have your leg on but if you have the control to put your leg on without going faster, the springier your jump will be.

Once your horse is going nicely over the crosses, think about the exit strategy, and don't stop riding when you have completed the grid. It would be nice to come out of the grid at the same speed and rhythm as that you go in with, and it would be very sensible at this stage to try to establish that he comes out *straight*. If your grid is against a fence, he will of course know which way he is going to turn when he lands. He cannot be labelled naughty if he leans in and tries to cut off in the direction in which he is going to turn, he is simply behaving naturally, and it is up to you to tell him how you want him to exit from the grid.

As you approach the end of the grid, ensure that you have a little more feel on the outside rein, and do keep your inside shoulder up. You don't want both of you on the slant and leaning in. Your horse should be encouraged to stay straight and only turn because you have asked him to, not because he anticipates the direction to take. Being level and feeling a little more outside rein will also have the added benefit of encouraging him to land on the correct lead. Although at this stage the leading leg isn't anything to worry too much about or concentrate on, making it easier for him to land on the correct leg is a very good habit for you to get into.

Quite often, after the grid, your horse may show a little 'woggle' or leap of enjoyment. One of my riders calls it 'dolphining' and I think that is very descriptive. It's definitely a display of enjoyment and something that won't upset an experienced rider, who will just find it amusing (Figure 3.3). A more novice rider, however, could find this unsettling and occasionally unseating; the bridging rein will help in this situation if the bridge is pushed down on his neck as the horse lands. He simply won't be able to get his head down so far that the innocent 'dolphining' develops into a full scale buck. If you are in this situation, keep your chin up as you don't want to collapse if he is already pulling you over his shoulder. The bridge will stop him getting too exuberant, and you must try very hard to keep him moving forward. If you try checking his forward movement to stop this behaviour, you might well find it could develop even more and turn into a bucking session; he will find it far more difficult for his 'dolphining' to become exaggerated if he is moving onwards. However much fun he is having, you don't want to end up on the ground!

Conversely, if the horse is silly and spooky and lacks confidence, both in himself and in his rider, you must encourage him to do the really basic stuff

Figure 3.3 Coming out of the grid, Stewie is terribly pleased with his efforts and Mary is amused.

as many times as it takes for him to relax and become willing. You have to look at the way the horse is going and decide how much to ask to get what you want. If you don't know the answer to that then don't advance too rapidly. Again, you need to think on your toes when training and remember that stopping an exercise in time could well avoid a serious problem for you and your horse's confidence. If the horse is going really well don't be tempted to move on and do too much at the point when he is getting tired. It's always sensible to stop too soon rather than too late.

You should have a plan for how you are going to build your grid, how you will alter it methodically, step by step, and what you hope to achieve in the first session, but be very prepared to amend that plan according to how the horse is going. You really won't know how he is going to take to it. If you follow the formula for building this novice series of grids, you will have plenty of exercises in hand. There is always more you can do. You will always be mentally one step ahead of him in the degree of difficulty of the exercise you plan to ask him to do; you know what you want to move on to next, he doesn't! If he finds the next exercise too demanding, just go back to the previous one, repeat it two or three times, making sure he does it well, and leave the next step for another day. You don't have to struggle to try to make him do all the novice exercises prescribed leading to a small combination in the first session; your only plan for the timescale should be 'no plan'.

Flare, the complete beginner

Did I say a plan? It is just as well there was no plan for Flare. This mare had not done anything at home except walk reluctantly over a pole, and it didn't look as if she was going to do much more this day (Figures 3.4 and 3.5). Diagram 2 shows the special grids I constructed for Flare.

She really was very resistant and the poles I put at the side of the grid spaces to encourage her to stay in a straight line didn't help. She came out over them backwards at such a rate and proceeded in reverse so quickly that she nearly sat down in temper.

She had been tricky and difficult to back, and has already demonstrated that she doesn't intend to work at all let alone start the grid work. However, Mary doesn't give up easily and persists with lots of leg to encourage Flare down the line. Flare soon gets used to the ground poles and when the poles were changed to very small crosses, she was almost too keen.

Flare has a very low concentration threshold and once she has done an exercise twice and is confident, she starts to get up to mischief. She is really sharp, but Mary is very patient and insists that Flare keeps working, even though her mood is erratic. It is so disappointing as she is obviously enjoying the new challenge, but she can't help being awkward when she thinks she knows it all (Figures 3.6–3.9).

Because she is actually doing the grid quite well, the last fence is altered very slightly to put a low horizontal pole behind the cross. It isn't any higher but she doesn't accept it gracefully. In spite of doing the earlier part of the grid well, when she spots there has been a change, she slams the brakes on (Figure 3.10).

Figures 3.4 and **3.5** Flare shows a distinct lack of enthusiasm for going forward.

Diagram 2   Grid for a complete and uncooperative beginner

Poles at open side of grid to stop horse running out

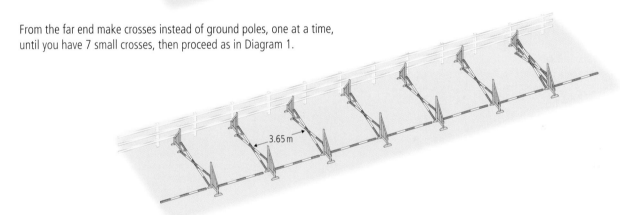

3.65 m

3.65 m

3.65 m

3.65 m

3.65 m

3.65 m

3.65 m
(12 ft/4 yd)

1 2 3 4 5 6 7

From the far end make crosses instead of ground poles, one at a time,
until you have 7 small crosses, then proceed as in Diagram 1.

3.65 m

This is the grid that Flare played up at and stopped at the end jump and so number 6 cross
was removed to give more room to take the horse in from the side and pop over the last jump
rather than her think refusing was an option.

3.65 m

The last jump is tiny, Flare did it easily and then dumped Mary when she approached it through the grid.
Sometimes horses regard missing poles as spooky as additional poles, and so you must remain wary if you take poles away.

Figure 3.6 Flare starts to look as if she is enjoying herself and Mary needs to be very positive about not allowing the mare to zoom off.

Figure 3.7 A few more times down the grid and Flare is looking good: relaxed and working well.

above left **Figure 3.8**
Unfortunately the good behaviour doesn't last and Mary has to sit tight!

above right **Figure 3.9**
I don't think this is happy 'dolphining'.

Figure 3.10 Flare is not going to be caught out and actually cooperate!

a

b

a

b

We cannot allow Flare to pick and choose what to do well, especially as this change in the last jump is minimal. The second last cross was, therefore, removed to give Mary room to go in to the grid from the side and pop out over the last jump (Figures 3.11a–d).

Mary has another go: the early grid goes well, but now Flare takes exception, not just to the last jump, but also to the gap where the second last cross has been removed, giving Mary no chance to stay in the saddle. It hasn't helped either that the saddle has slipped forwards due to Flare's strenuous efforts! (Figures 3.12a–f.)

top row **Figures 3.11a–d** Why couldn't she do it the first time?

middle row and right **Figures 3.12a–f** Ouch! Even the best of riders hit the deck sometimes.

c

d

c

d

e

f

Flare's bad behaviour leaves her feeling triumphant (Figures 3.13 and 3.14) but Mary isn't a quitter, that's why she's been asked to ride this sharp little mare, and once they are reunited, Flare is given no option but to do it properly (Figures 3.15a and b).

Although Flare has had fun and games on the grid, eventually she has cooperated and realized that, for all her shenanigans, she is not going to have things all her own way. Her performance through the grid has only been passable and she is going to need lots of consistent work to encourage her not just to jump but also to behave. She hasn't won the fairly major argument because Mary got on again and achieved the desired result, but had Mary been badly hurt and had to leave it for the day, Flare would have prevailed; imagine what that would have done for her ego.

Figure 3.13 Oops! I appear to have lost my rider.

Figure 3.14 Would someone mind sorting out my reins?

a

b

You can see from her demeanour that she has mostly enjoyed what she's done, her ears are pricked and her work has occasionally looked quite promising but she likes to play up and be naughty even more. Mary has done a marvellous job in spite of being thrown on the ground, and Flare has learned that she must do as she's asked in the end. The result was not as good as it could have been, but this mare is very strong willed and reluctant to do anything the first time she's asked.

You can now see why I don't want a novice rider starting on a novice horse.

Novice-horse grid 2

Cahan the naughty novice

Zena's horse Cahan is one of the naughtiest horses I have ever trained. She is nappy, uncooperative and bad tempered, and there was a doubt that this mare would ever be able to compete (Figure 3.16).

Cahan had jumped a few poles at home – usually with a lead – and a few small obstacles when out hacking. Zena wanted to get her going properly so that she could compete in some local show jumping and eventing. She wanted to improve, both her riding and the horse.

When I first saw Cahan, it was a major issue for her to be able to step over a pole on the floor; sometimes it still is. After her first traumatic session when Zena had been thrown to the ground three times, she was quite matter of fact about the problems and said that she supposed I wouldn't want to see her again. I was amazed that she wanted to continue, as the mare was so obviously much more than a normal challenge. I suppose it was Zena's attitude that encouraged me to encourage her. She just put up with everything, even after being flung off, and always blamed herself for doing something wrong or unacceptable to the mare. Her sympathy towards the mare's obvious hang-ups was quite touching. Cahan was a rejected racehorse and I suspect if

opposite page
Figures 3.15a and **b**
Mary stays well back in a position from which she can insist that Flare stays up in front of her. Her hands may be a little high, but she is riding in a safety position as she doesn't intend to be shot off again.

Figure 3.16 Cahan's first reaction to any request is always to say no!

Zena hadn't taken her on, she would have soon been dispatched for meat. Zena really believed that with lots of patience she could make a difference to the horse, but I certainly had more doubts.

When Zena said that she supposed I wouldn't want to see her again, it was very tempting to answer her with, 'No, I don't think you'll ever get her going well enough'. But as long as the rider wanted to keep trying, then I had to admire her commitment. I have 100 per cent faith in my grid-work exercises; they have helped every horse I've ever trained to jump better, but if we couldn't even get Cahan near a grid…?

It looked at first as if there was going to be no progress whatsoever and Zena said that she would quite understand if I didn't want to carry on.

In fact, it looked as if we were going to make this disobedient horse even worse behaved than she already was. Putting her rider on the ground three times in one session does not constitute minor mis-understandings; this spinning, bucking, rearing horse really meant to get rid of her rider (Figures 3.17a and b). And that was when she was nowhere near a jump but just while warming up. She refused to walk over a pole, refused, indeed, to go forward at all, reversing at high speed always, uncannily, in my direction; Cahan kept me on my toes as I dodged her flying back feet!

I had to rethink my strategy entirely as there was no way we were going to encourage her down my normal starter grid of 7 tiny crosses. She simply wouldn't consider going near it. I had to forget how

Figures 3.17a and **b** Cahan definitely has a mind of her own.

I normally work and devise a whole new approach that was tailor-made to overcome her stubbornness. Usually, my step-by-step methods work easily and, most importantly, encourage confidence and co-operation in the majority of the starter horses I see. It was never going to work in this case.

But there is always a way, you just have to work it out, however long it takes. It took me a little trial and error to think of something that would work effectively so that Zena could do what she set out to do and still stay in the saddle. In the end, there was no deep-rooted horsy knowledge I could dredge up to deal with this; plain common sense prevailed. If the mare wouldn't go to the poles, then the poles were going to go to her! (Diagram 3)

Diagram 3 The empty-pair-of-wings grid

A very difficult horse should be walked through empty wings and then be boxed in the middle of the grid with ground poles. The only way he can get out is over a pole.

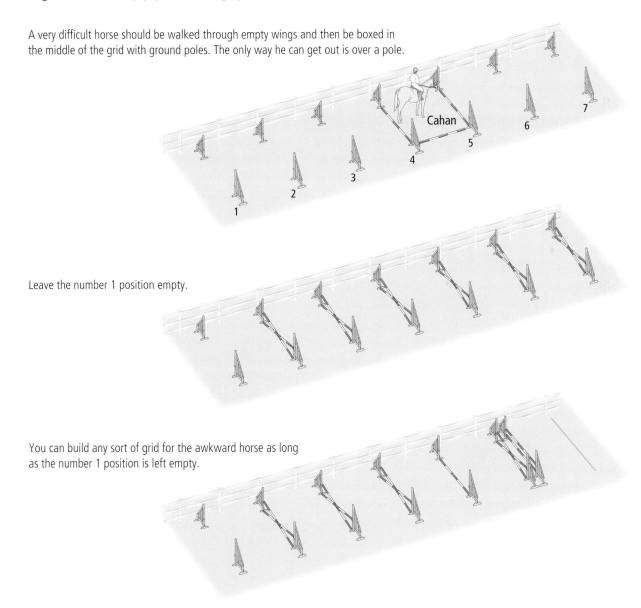

Leave the number 1 position empty.

You can build any sort of grid for the awkward horse as long as the number 1 position is left empty.

All the poles on the grid were removed, leaving just the wings standing; Zena rode the suspicious mare halfway down the line, and halted. Before she could go into reverse, poles were placed on the ground behind, in front and to the side of her away from the fence, so to go anywhere, she would have to actually step over a pole (Figure 3.18).

Eventually it worked as she was nagged and cajoled to just move. At this stage it really didn't matter how much time it took as long as she did what she was asked. I suppose she cooperated in the end because she became bored. Using the stick was not an option. Until Cahan learned to go because Zena kicked her forward, we would get nowhere. We repeated this literally dozens of times until she was so fed up she just gave in and walked over the poles nicely (Figure 3.19).

Once Cahan had gone over the 2 poles in the middle of the grid, I thought we could take a chance on adding some more at the end, and then some towards the front of the grid until she was walking reasonably well over 6 poles between the wings set at the 3.35–3.65 m (11–12 ft) bounce distance. This distance is ideal for her three walk strides, two trot strides and one canter stride. As Cahan was such a reluctant horse, the shorter distance suited her better. When she was walking forward consistently well enough, she did three nice strides between the poles. When she was being crabby, it could have been as many as five or six strides. When the final pole was added at the first wings to make 7 in a row, she refused point blank to approach the line. Could she count? I think not, because when a 7th pole was placed at the far end of the grid, although it had no wings, she was fine. She just would not consider tackling that first 'jump' or step into a grid. As long as the first wings were empty she was happy and cooperative (Figure 3.20). She went down the poles comfortably in trot, then in canter, with no problems at all. Once she consented to go forward,

below left **Figure 3.18** Cahan looks for an easy way out.

below **Figure 3.19** Even now, if Cahan is in a mumpy mood we still sometimes have to start her schooling session with this exercise before we can progress any further. Patience prevails in the end and here she looks quite happy stepping out over the box of poles.

I could start to build the grid up gradually to the sort of starter grid with cross poles that I like to use; minus the poles at the first jump!

After we had built up to the crosses, we progressed to the small combination that we did for Steph's first lesson. The novice-rider exercise is the ideal first-session grid for novice horses too. Cahan was fine as long as Zena consistently continued to nag and hold the contact, and the jumps were small (Figures 3.21a and b).

right **Figure 3.20** The empty-pair-of-wings grid. Even now, Cahan will not go down a grid straight away unless the first pair of wings is poleless!

b

a

I could see that it was difficult for Zena to balance well enough to be quite as effective as Cahan needed. She needed to use more leg, have more confidence to look up, to keep hold of the contact, and to be ready to sense when Cahan was about to play up. Once she had sensed impending disobedience, Zena then needed to be quick enough and strong enough to circumvent this tendency: all the usual requirements for better jumping, but Cahan didn't make it easy.

Figures 3.21a and **b** Once in through the empty pair of wings, Cahan makes a really good job of the grid and finishes with a happy jump out.

Obviously these things needed to be sorted out very soon, as the mare was quite difficult enough without rider error giving her an excuse to nap, run out or dump her partner. Despite this, the first efforts at a 'proper' grid were starting to look promising. We hadn't prevailed easily, it had taken a lot of time, effort and patience, but we had managed to eventually do what we wanted, even if we built up to it stealthily. Now the tricky bit was to try going through the grid the other way. It is always sensible to start the grid exercises going towards the gate because, even if your horse is not nappy, many have an unmistakable bias for returning to the exit corner, and sometimes this bias can be very helpful in encouraging a 'sticky' horse to get going.

Having started Cahan in the direction of the gate, I expected trouble as soon as the direction was reversed, and had the empty wings ready. Surprisingly, Cahan went down the grid like a veteran, all nonsense forgotten as she began to enjoy what she was doing. We asked her to do it again, and then decided that that was enough for the first session.

Initially an honest answer to Zena's question about whether I was prepared to carry on with the two of them would have been 'I don't know' because it was impossible to predict how Cahan was going to progress, but I felt it was worth carrying on for two reasons. The mare enjoyed her jumping

when she forgot about bad behaviour and, when circumstances were right, she looked good in the air. Nowadays, she looks good more often than not. (Figures 3.22a–c)

We compromised with Cahan two years ago when we started working together, and we still do now. Zena sometimes comes home from a show with loads of rosettes, sometimes she comes away with nothing but we keep on with the grid work between outings to reaffirm the balance of power.

These days we can start off more conventionally and the mare really enjoys her jumping exercises; and we still always start the grid with the empty wings if Cahan is in a particularly awkward frame of mind. If she seems amenable we may start with a very small first jump instead, small enough for Cahan to take from a standstill. If it looks like turning into a battle, I just take the first jump poles away with her still standing there. She must not think that turning or napping will give her the results she desires.

Turning away after a refusal is not an option on

c

b

the grid. The plastic poles are safe enough to be kicked about without hurting the horse, and they can be put at ground level or removed with the horse still facing the whole grid. If you turn away and have another go, the horse learns that this can be an option, and will remember that for future battles.

If Cahan is really awkward and goes into reverse, she gets a smack with a stick on her bottom. Not too hard, just enough to humiliate rather than hurt her. As soon as she stops reversing, the stick is kept still and Zena has to boot and kick to make her go forward again. I *never* let anyone use a stick to make the horse go forward, but I do think a tap on the bum is justified when your horse is really napping backwards. So *be absolutely clear:* it is a smack for being naughty, but a kick to resume normal action.

Cahan taught me a lot, as the empty-pair-of-wings grid has worked superbly well for other nappy horses, and not all of them novices. A Grade A show jumper who had started refusing came to me for some grid work to try to get him going

again. He was adamant that he wouldn't work through a grid. As soon as the poles from the first wings were removed he was fine, and was no more trouble. Once his grid work was re-established, he stopped stopping and started to enjoy the job again.

The empty wings are a very good way to kick start horses and remind them that it is best to do as they are asked. It is no great hardship to pass between some empty wings and get going. I would not begin to try to understand why this works, it is not a situation or a method that should be analysed; it is just useful to know it can be used as an alternative when a horse is being very difficult and uncooperative.

If Cahan, or any other tricky horse, has a break from this work, or they are in a particularly bad mood, the empty wings seem to sort it out. It just avoids all the napping and naughtiness which characterizes the stubborn attitude some horses develop when asked to do something, even when they actually enjoy the job. They just enjoy the power struggle more.

a

Figures 3.22 a–c a) The canter pole produces exactly the right power from her back end; b) in the middle of the grid in fine style; c) jumping out of the grid: size doesn't matter when Cahan cooperates, and now she looks as if she's really enjoying her jumping.

It is so exhausting for Zena, Cahan, and my patience to always have to fight. As long as there is a key method to making the work easier, it's just sensible to use it. Zena is not a young and silly teenager, but has a real affection for this awkward mare. Not only does she want to jump with her, she also wants to jump better. She does, therefore, keep coming for training; we devise more and more complicated exercises to keep the mare interested, and if she really kicks off on a major tantrum, we try for a compromise, rather than an outright battle (Figures 3.23a and b). And, importantly, Cahan also seems to enjoy what she does when she can bring herself to cooperate.

She actually likes to jump and is now quite extravagant in the air. If she allows Zena to ride her instead of arguing with her, they both have a lot of fun. But she can still manage to surprise me, although I know most of her foibles pretty well. Recently she caught me out by refusing to go near a very plain fence on the grass (Fence 1 on the practice course); it was simply a cross with two horizontal poles, just like the grid fences she is used to (Figures 3.24). The jump immediately after it at number 2 was a bright wall which she sailed over

Figures 3.23a and **b** a) You must be joking; b) Well, if you insist!

a

b

with no hesitation. She jumped that fence nicely two or three times, but still utterly refused to contemplate the plain poles. In exasperation I removed the poles from the preceding jump, leaving poleless wings to pass through and, with perseverance, Zena soon has Cahan back on track (Figures 3.25a–c).

Cahan doesn't nap at strange obstacles like water trays. I would have bet on her throwing a tantrum at new challenges, not because of a lack of ability, but because of pure disobedience and I would have lost. She doesn't use a new jump as an excuse to play up; she plays up because she chooses to, with no external reason. A jump is just a jump to her, and she doesn't differentiate between them if we introduce any new fences (Figure 3.26).

The only time Cahan would be difficult on a course because of the appearance of the jumps is if Zena doesn't like the look of something and doesn't ride as consistently as normal.

All the grids we do now build up to more serious fences, and she is quite happy to pop over 1.05 m (3 ft 6 in) in nice style. She is not a bit disconcerted by the size of the fences and she snaps up her legs and makes a nice shape in the air. The conventional grids that other horses find straightforward are now very easy for her too, and it gives me a chance to concentrate on Zena's shortcomings.

Because Cahan has been so difficult, it has been hard for Zena to ride her effectively all the time. Sometimes, even when the horse is in a cooperative frame of mind, Zena has lost the initiative by not keeping a consistent contact. In the early stages, things had to be so basic to actually get Cahan through a grid, that refining and improving Zena's riding was put on hold. If she had developed a consistent contact sooner, there would have been fewer problems with the mare, and progress might have been easier. But it is difficult to keep hold of the contact when a mare is disappearing from underneath you backwards!

Although Cahan has plenty of jump and scope she can't (not won't) operate over more demanding fences if she loses impulsion. Zena has always had to use a very strong and consistent leg just to get Cahan to move, so she is used to doing that. More issues occur now because she finds it difficult to support and contain Cahan's energy with a consistent contact. If she drops her hands at the take-off point, the mare immediately loses all the impulsion generated, which makes it difficult for her to jump and so she doesn't! She won't be helpful and keep going without enough 'ping', and why should she?

Figures 3.24 Every bone in Cahan's body is saying 'No, and I mean no'.

Figures 3.25a–c a) What a palaver at fence number 1 on the practice course! Where's the jump gone? The ground poles keep Cahan square to the empty pair of wings; b) Zena has insisted Cahan should behave and has managed to drive her hind leg so far under her that it would be very difficult to stop; c) Zena has Cahan working properly again.

c

b   a

The mare soon realizes that any inconsistency with the contact to her bit means she can play up and give her rider a hard time. Sometimes she deliberately and suddenly drops her nose to her chest to lose the contact. Unless Zena very rapidly uses even more leg to make her pick up the contact again, Cahan is in charge!

The rider owes it to the horse to make the jumping job as easy as possible. So many refusals are caused by the rider very suddenly, at the most crucial point of take-off, making it hard for the horse to get in the air. They release the energy and instantaneously, in that last split second, the horse finds the power required to jump fizzles away and so he stops.

opposite **Figure 3.26** Cahan sails over all the other new and bright fences without a second look, making a lovely job of the planks – number 4 of the practice course. I can't explain why she stopped at the green poles. I suppose it was because she wanted to, another little power struggle. All I can do is try to overcome her silliness or disobedience so that she doesn't feel she has got the better of Zena.

What do you do if your trainer says you've dropped your hands and you know you haven't? Zena didn't ask me this question, she asked the friend who recommended me as a trainer. And the friend said 'If I was you, I would change my mind' I heard about this from both ladies a few weeks later.

When you are trying your best, it is indeed disheartening to be told you are doing the wrong thing, especially when you remain unconvinced. But the only way to learn to jump better is to listen to advice and to practise. Work on the problem, and be honest enough to admit that perhaps the trainer might be right. The only way for the trainer to prove the point is to work the rider over basic grids and keep pushing them to look up and keep hold of the contact. Gradually, the principle of enough leg to a supporting hand will become more automatic, and the stops or run-outs will happen less frequently.

This very positive attitude to holding and keeping the contact really goes against any normal instinct. Whatever other sport you do, you try to improve your performance by going faster, using more effort, giving yourself more pressure, and usually by leaning forward and 'going for it'. This is the wrong thing to do with horses.

Working through various grids will help you to consistently jump better. The progressive nature of the exercises will help you to be confident. Even the tiniest grids should be taken seriously, and you should work hard to produce the maximum amount of impulsion you can. Then you must contain that impulsion, not just up to the jump, but also when riding away from it on the other side in preparation for the next obstacle. Once you have as much impulsion as you can gather, there is no more. If you wriggle about and try and get up more steam when the jumps get bigger, all you will do is distract the horse and confuse him as you change into a different person. To jump bigger fences, you don't need to change your mode of riding and try harder because you should already be doing enough over the smaller fences. Your horse will make the extra effort because he can, because you have kept up the impulsion and contact, and because you don't change things and confuse him.

To jump better, the rider needs to do things properly from the beginning and then always try to do *the same* whatever jump is facing them.

It was easy for Cahan to jump small grids and fences once Zena actually got the mare to move forward. As the mare learned to enjoy what she was doing, a little enthusiasm crept in and, if Zena wasn't riding quite perfectly, she would sometimes help her out by skipping on down the line voluntarily; but not for long. As soon as Zena started to take her for granted, and it was *always* when they were going well, she would ease her hands to take off, and Cahan would stop.

The only way you are going to convince the rider to wait and keep hold is to point out that when things go wrong, they will put themselves right again if next time the rider holds the contact for a little bit longer. Zena's main obstacles to jumping

better were her kind attitude, and an old-fashioned belief that she should throw her reins away over the jump, 'freeing the horse's head and neck so she could use herself'. Unfortunately she ended up freeing herself to get up to mischief! And this method usually ended with Zena hitting the floor. It was difficult to persuade Zena to look up and hold the contact consistently, as well as remembering to keep enough leg on the mare to make her behave.

The very nature of the exercise and consistency required to ride a conventional grid well help both of them to do better. As the rider makes fewer mistakes, the mare goes better and better and if things are going smoothly, it should be easy to remember why. If Zena forgets, however, and doesn't use enough leg and either looks for a stride or tips forward too far and too early, she doesn't get away with it. Cahan will stop and run backwards in an instant if she isn't given the right aids to produce enough impulsion to make the job easy.

Cahan rarely helps Zena out freely but, if things are right for her, nowadays she usually does pretty well.

When Zena takes Cahan to shows, the effects of her training last for two or three outings before she or Cahan allow bad habits to creep in again, and they both need the reminder of the grid work to set them back on the straight and narrow.

If Cahan goes badly at the schooling session, Zena *has* to persist with the work, however long it takes until Cahan begins to cooperate again. Even if she only does one exercise properly, Zena has to reach the point when she asks and Cahan says 'OK', although attempting more progression on that particular day would be unwise.

Whenever Cahan is presented with a new challenge on the grid, she still prefers to say 'No' the first time, and so Zena compromises by changing things only when Cahan is working well and enjoying herself.

If all went too smoothly I would be suspicious and wonder what she might be hatching, as her whole being seems to concentrate on initiating a power struggle. She is still very much a novice and although she isn't asked to work too hard (unless she starts a major battle) and jump difficult fences, she is nagged until she cooperates once more. If she allowed herself to progress at a more conventional rate instead of making a major issue over each new step introduced, she would be doing really well in the ring (Figures 3.27a and b). Most horses given her opportunities to learn would be jumping in more demanding classes and be doing really well with lots more rosettes to their names.

Zena's patience with this tricky mare is admirable, and I am delighted to help her improve, but if we hadn't used the grid-work methods, I don't think she would be jumpable at all. It is only her temperament that holds her back, not her undoubted ability, and less awkward horses are doing in three months what Cahan has taken two years to achieve. If Zena hadn't persisted with the grid work, I really think she should have given up. The grid work gave her the confidence to recognize that she wasn't being unreasonable with the mare and it is now a constant reminder not only to encourage Cahan to jump better but also to behave herself as well.

a

Figures 3.27a and **b** Show day. a) Cahan demonstrates why she wears a red ribbon; b) Once she's persuaded to get in the ring, however, her jumping is impeccable.

b

4 The roller-coaster grid

I like to use the roller-coaster grid (Diagram 4) to encourage consistency, particularly with the larger horses who have done the 7 conventional crosses often enough to find it easy. The number 1, 3, 5 and 7 cross poles go up and the alternate number 2, 4 and 6 cross poles go down. In this way I am trying to encourage the horse's hoof prints to be right in the middle of the distances, in exactly the same place as on the control grid, i.e. the grid with all the crosses at the same height. It is an exercise in consistency, to try to make a horse light and airy, going 'up' rather than long, low and flat, whatever size of fence you are jumping. If you don't support a horse enough through the grid and allow him to follow his natural inclinations, he will go long and flat at the small crosses and then prop and have to back off to jump the high crosses. If you are doing this exercise correctly the horse should jump all the crosses from the same take-off point in the middle of the distances, whether they are high or low. The stride length should feel the same but with higher alternate jumps all the way through. (Figure 4.1)

Q *Are the canter poles placed on the way in to the grid to act as placing poles?*

A *No, they are a guide to tell you if you are riding the last two or three strides of the approach in exactly the same way.*

Figure 4.1 Val and Maizie are dead straight over this uninviting and difficult roller-coaster grid.

Diagram 4 The roller-coaster grid

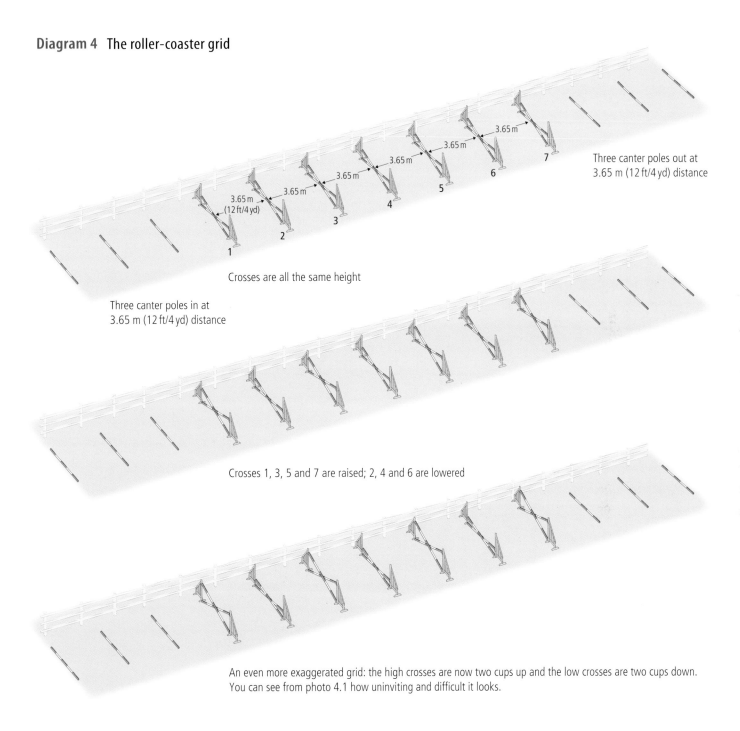

Three canter poles out at
3.65 m (12 ft/4 yd) distance

Crosses are all the same height

Three canter poles in at
3.65 m (12 ft/4 yd) distance

Crosses 1, 3, 5 and 7 are raised; 2, 4 and 6 are lowered

An even more exaggerated grid: the high crosses are now two cups up and the low crosses are two cups down. You can see from photo 4.1 how uninviting and difficult it looks.

The canter poles are there to make sure you are consistent, both when going in to the grid and leaving it. The canter poles going in are not to be used, or thought of, as placing poles, it doesn't matter whether the poles are in the middle of your horse's stride or not. When you jump a course it is unlikely that you will meet every jump at the take-off point you want, and you need to be aware that as long as you keep the same rhythm and impulsion going in to the fence, at whatever point you arrive, your horse will be able to use all that power and energy to make a good job of it, no matter where he actually leaves the ground. What you perceive to be the perfect take-off point is irrelevant to your horse. All he knows is whether the last stride is a well-ridden stride or not, i.e. if you continue to ride in the same way, he will adjust his stride to jump well. If you mess about and change your mode of riding when you see you are going to be a little deep in to the fence or either a little or long way off it and you aren't happy, your natural inclination is to stop riding and pushing. The horse then has to try to cope with reduced energy. If riders have a tendency to peer down to try to look for their stride they either flap and panic if they are too far off the fence or stop riding completely if they are going in too deep to it. This is why I am so keen for riders to look up and not down on the approach to a fence.

Looking down for a stride inevitably encourages you to be too forward in your position, making the situation worse as your weight is too far over his shoulder to give you a springy takeoff. You will probably also give your hands and contact away when the horse most needs to rely on your consistency and support. You must recognize that for the horse there is really no wrong take-off stride if you keep working. If the rhythm is consistent, regardless of the stride, he will jump anything up to around 1.05 m (3 ft 6 in) or so comfortably, and probably a lot more. I repeat, if you don't ride the last stride

because you think a horse is going to arrive at the wrong place for takeoff, he won't be given enough impulsion to get on with the job.

The poles on the way in to the grid – the 'in' poles – are there to encourage you to push and ride the last two or three strides before the jump *in the same way*. For example, if you are short over the first canter pole I want you to be short over the second pole too. Don't try to make up ground to get the next pole in the middle of his stride. You must not try to organize your horse to jump them perfectly. However you go over the first pole, the second pole should be in the same place on his stride. It is called **consistency** and it's what your horse needs most to help his approach. Just keep riding the same way; if you don't, the canter poles will act as a guide to let you know whether or not you are keeping your impulsion. If you keep pushing and supporting all the way to the jump, wherever you take off, you will jump it well and land in balance for the rest of the exercise.

> **Q** *Why are there poles on the landing side of the grid?*
>
> **A** *The 'out' canter poles are there to let you know if you are landing and riding away rather than landing and letting your horse take the initiative.*

A horse can choose to be lazy or over-keen – zoomy – and the 'out' poles will let you know immediately so that you can do something about it. These poles do need to be in the middle of his stride. When you land over the last obstacle you need to re-establish your strong and active canter, and if you need to steady or push to do this, the poles will let you know. When you jump related distances round a course, you will always be able to ride them so much better if the canter is strong and active away from every jump. The poles are not there to make your horse work better after landing. They are there to let you know exactly how much you need to do to ride away properly, with lots of energy and impulsion instead of being too stuffy and short or too fast and long and flat. Your horse might be extravagant and do more than necessary, jumping the poles two or three times instead of just cantering over them, but he will soon not bother to do that and will ignore them. Then it's up to you to keep up the power and consistency of the stride. (Figure 4.2)

You do not have to be perfect over the canter poles into the grid but when you come out you should be spot on. You should have that up-tempo canter that the poles produce and you should land in the middle of the distance with the poles in the middle of your stride. If you are too fast and flat, you will be too close to them. If you don't use enough leg when you come out you will be dropping a bit short of the poles. Let the poles help you get away from the jump better, don't look at them as an extra hazard; they are there only as a guide.

George and Karen

George is a *big* boy. He is a hunter who competes a bit in the summer and so he needs a grid to lighten him up and keep him springy (Figure 4.3). Now crosses 1, 3, 5 and 7 are put up and crosses 2, 4 and 6 are put down so that they are asymmetric and uninviting (Figure 4.4).

The horse should still jump through and land with his feet in the same position as in the control grid (Figure 4.5). It is an exercise in consistency and you should treat the small crosses as seriously as the big ones. The small crosses are not there to provide a breathing space; they are there to be ridden.

When the jumps are more exaggerated, i.e. with the high crosses being even higher and the low crosses even lower, the consistency is even more difficult to achieve (Figures 4.6a–c) especially when you have to remember to work over the canter poles too. Once the horse has come out of the grid neither of you must relax; the canter away must still be ridden.

Figure 4.2 Here Val and Maizie are surprisingly 'airy' over the canter poles out of the control grid. Maizie is experienced with grids but the canter poles surprised her and made her do more work than necessary but she soon settled down over the poles and Val was able to treat them as an aid to establishing a strong and active canter and riding away from the grid properly, instead of extra jumps.

above left **Figure 4.3**
Karen and George are
very straight on the
control grid and ready
to make a good job of
the canter poles away.

above right **Figure 4.4**
George is unfazed by
the uninviting
appearance of the
roller-coaster grid.

Figure 4.5 George is
landing spot on in the
middle of the distance.
Karen is looking up and
not allowing George to
tug her too far forward.

Figures 4.6a–c a) and b) George taking both low and high crosses equally well; c) note how effective this grid is: George is in perfect balance.

George is asked to practise the three-stride distance in the arena to see if the work he has done on the grid has been effective. When he has a bit more open space, he gets very enthusiastic and makes up too much ground (Figure 4.7).

The canter poles are used between the fences to remind Karen how much she has to steady him and not let him charge on, which he has a tendency to do, and Karen has to deal with this (Figure 4.8).

All this work with the grids and canter poles enables Karen and George to put in a good performance on show day (Figures 4.9a and b).

Figure 4.7 George's keenness carries him forward on the related distance of four strides and he gets a little close to the jump. Although he jumped very well, he was still a little deep.

Figure 4.8 The canter poles remind Karen just how much hold she needs to keep George's stride regular and conventional and steady on a related distance.

a

b

above, left and right **Figures 4.9a** and **b** Show day: Karen gathers George up as if the canter poles are there, both through a) the double and b) on to the parallel.

Maizie and Val

Maizie is also a big horse and, as with Karen and George, the roller-coaster grid will encourage Val to ask Maizie to work upwards from her stride rather than along (Figure 4.10).

The roller-coaster grid is absolutely perfect for helping horses and riders cope with any change of level such as banks, drops or steps. Because the grid actively encourages the rider to produce the consistent impulsion and feel, whatever height the horse is expected to jump, low or high, going up or down a level should not be a problem.

The distance on top of the bank is a perfect two strides. Because the grid has enabled Val to feel and practise the difference between low and high crosses with Maizie jumping higher, then lower again, absorbing the different levels should be no problem. Val must ride the bank as if she expects the rails to be on level ground. It is up to Maizie to deal with the different levels of landing, both up and down.

Figure 4.10 Val is a little too far forward but hanging onto the contact to help Maizie to land after the low cross and jump perfectly from the middle of the distance.

If Val rides her as consistently as she did on the grid it is easy for Maizie to sort this out for herself. If Val tries to help and 'lift' her horse up or exaggerate her position to stay back too far when coming down, her horse will be distracted. Maizie can see what she has to do, and as long as Val maintains her power, whether she's going up or coming down, Maizie will find it easy (Figures 4.11a and b).

Val then moves on to the show jumps set up on

the grass specifically for course practice (Diagram 5). This practice course can feature most of the problems riders are likely to find at a show and is a natural progression from any of the grids in the following chapters.

When Val and Maizie work over the practice course, they both find it harder to land from a fence and immediately re-establish the strong canter. When they tried the related distances on the course of show jumps, Val didn't have quite enough leg on and wasn't as consistent as she was on the grid (Figure 4.12).

b

a

Figures 4.11a and b Immediately after work over the grid, Val and Maizie are jumping nimbly, cleanly and actively onto and off the bank and rails.

Diagram 5 The practice course on grass

Plan

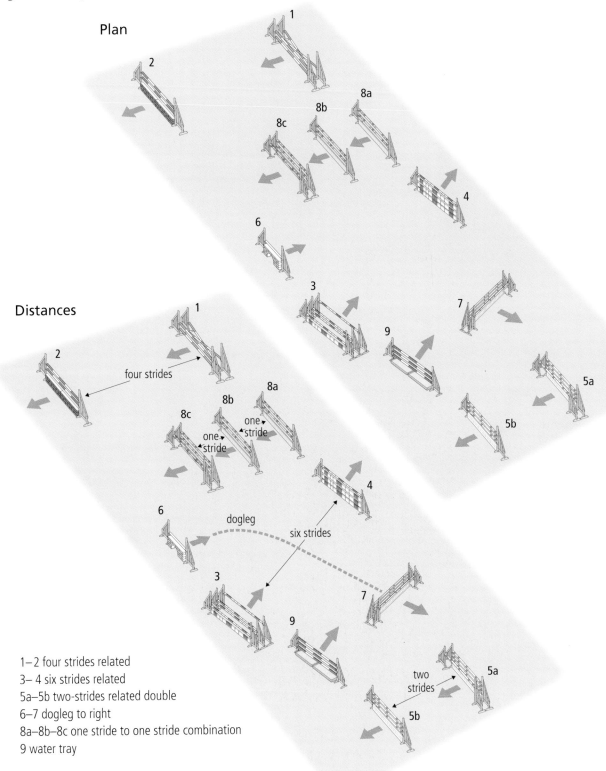

Distances

1–2 four strides related
3–4 six strides related
5a–5b two-strides related double
6–7 dogleg to right
8a–8b–8c one stride to one stride combination
9 water tray

Figure 4.12 Maizie is putting in an extra stride on this four-stride distance between fences 1 and 2 of the practice course and getting much too deep in to the fence.

below **Figures 4.13a and b** If you compare these photos to 4.12 you can see what a difference the canter poles make to the canter power and therefore the jump: it is lighter and much more active.

b

a

Because Val needs to make Maizie work harder after landing not faster, four canter poles were put down. Val used them to recognize how quick she needed to be after the first jump, how much more leg she needed to use and how easily Maizie can cover the ground when she's working. There is no need to switch to a different mode of riding because she is jumping a course. The canter poles demonstrated to Val know just how much she needs to

push to hold the rhythm, impulsion and length of stride to the next jump.

Once Maizie was encouraged to work immediately from her landing stride, she found the distance just right for her four working strides. Providing Val rode her as positively as she did on the grid, whatever the first jump was like and however she landed, and provided Val insisted that she work, it was easy (Figures 4.13a and b).

After the canter poles were removed, Val had established a feel for the level of work she needed to maintain and Maizie's canter approach was vastly improved (Figure 4.14). Val just needed that little bit of extra help from the canter poles to help her recognize just how much she needed to do to ride different fences as effectively as her grid work.

When you practise at home, you must remember that grid work and courses are not two separate exercises. Carry the grid work with you when you tackle different jumps or whole courses, your horse will only be confused if you change the way you ride or the power you produce. Just because you have more room round a course and the jumping efforts aren't so concentrated, it is no reason to slacken off the amount of energy you generate. It must stay the same to give your horse confidence and impulsion whatever you ask him to jump. If you turn into a different rider, you will turn him into a different horse. And you won't like what you get!

Figure 4.14 A great canter approach to jump number 2 on the practice course with no poles to help.

Once Val had recognized and established just how hard she needed to work over different obstacles, everything fell into place. She was much quicker to work when she landed and made everything easy for Maizie. The partnership carried the good work forward to the practice course (Figure 4.15) and to the show ring (Figure 4.16).

left **Figure 4.15** Committed, active and straight down the middle at this very bright combination: number 8 on the practice course.

above **Figure 4.16** Val is producing a top quality canter at a show, as good a canter as if the poles were there to help her.

5 The stay-straight grid

Q *How can I help my horse jump straight?*

A *Nearly all horses have a bias to jump to one side or the other, and careful early training will go a long way to prevent this becoming too pronounced.*

Young horses have a tendency to hang towards the fence as they do their grid work, it is very much a security thing, and when the fence happens to be on the side they favour hanging to anyway, the habit is very obvious. When the fence is on the other side, the bias to hang to one side and the lure of the security of the fence often cancels out the tendency and the horse goes straight down the middle. However it isn't that simple to correct, you can't work on only one rein in order to stay straight!

With the straight grids, sometimes raising the height of the cross on the favoured side can be effective, but not always (Figure 5.1).

If the horse is well practised in the art of deciding how he wishes to proceed, you must try a somewhat more positive method to help the steering. And whatever else you are working on the grid for, the following method of keeping the horse in the middle will work without fail. You don't want a wrestling match with the reins to try to steer for the middle; you don't want to try to force him to go where you want if you can manage to improve the situation without pulling him about too strongly.

Figure 5.1 Leo is not going to be encouraged to the middle by the higher end of the cross; he just picks his feet up more.

You want to encourage the right sort of feel and directional cooperation without a battle. Diagonal or V poles on the *ground* will supply you with everything you need.

Diagonal ground poles

Gus and Vanessa

Vanessa has problems with Gus jumping to the left (Figure 5.2). Diagonal poles on the ground between each cross pointing towards the centre of the cross (Diagram 6) will guide Gus towards the middle and

Diagram 6 The stay-straight grid

Make the cross higher on the side to which the horse hangs.

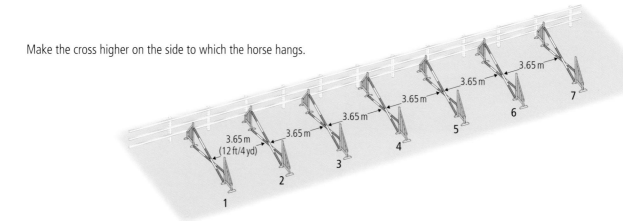

If the first grid doesn't work, then diagonal guide poles will do the trick.
Don't forget to move them to the opposite side when you turn the grid round.

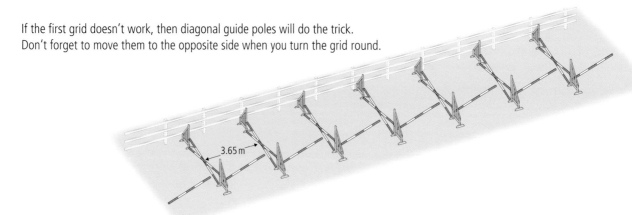

When you build the grid up and have non-jumping strides,
use two diagonal poles in the gap.

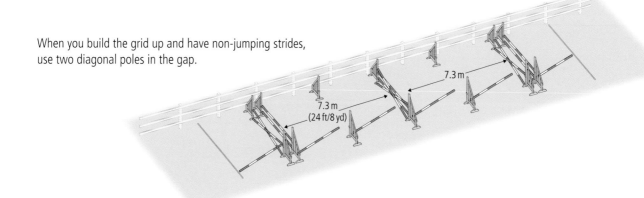

help make Vanessa a little more aware of what she should be encouraging (Figure 5.3).

When Gus has repeated the exercise several times, Vanessa starts to get more of a feel for riding him straighter, but he is just looking for an opportunity to revert to his old ways when she tries to work round a course (Figures 5.4a and b).

It is very naughty of him to try to take charge, and how much easier it would be for them both if he didn't keep trying to assert himself. Vanessa *must* be quicker to keep hold when she lands to try to prevent this happening. Once she has softened her contact as they land, he looks on it as a weakness and goes off at a tangent. If Vanessa hauls on the reins and fights to try to keep him straight when it is too late, she will get a lot more resistance, he may even run out or refuse; the long-term aim is, therefore, to nag persistently until the horse cooperates rather than bullying him to achieve a quick fix that will not give a long-term result. The short-term solution is to use some V poles on the ground between the jumps (Figure 5.5).

Figure 5.2 In spite of Vanessa's best efforts, Gus is determined to jump to his left.

Figure 5.3 The diagonal poles bring about an immediate improvement, although Vanessa must be aware that leaning her weight to the middle won't help. She must try very hard to be level. He must learn to straighten up under her.

a

above and right **Figures 5.4a** and **b** Although Vanessa jumps in to this two-stride double (jump number 5 on the practice course) perfectly in the middle (a), he seizes the initiative on the two non-jumping strides to cut across to the left (b).

b

Figure 5.5 The poles are placed on the ground to form a guiding V to help, not force, Vanessa to be quick enough to hold, support and steer across the distance in a straight line.

V poles

A few guiding V poles are very effective as they give the rider a positive idea about just how much they should be imposing their will. There is no need at all for Gus to veer across to the left so violently when he has jumped the first part properly, and Vanessa needs a little help to recognize how much she has to do to keep him central over both parts. She must really focus on looking for the middle of the jump and keep her hands level, very supportive and tucked into Gus's neck with her knuckles almost pointing to where she wants him to go. She must boot and drive him into this contact so there

is no opportunity for him to drop behind the bit and waver (Figure 5.6). The poles will give her a bit of breathing space and guidance and she will be able to start to recognize how much and how quickly she needs to ride on when landing to prevent this lateral dive.

Vanessa must beaver away with her grid work, diagonal poles and V poles until Gus begins to understand that he is not going to be allowed to hang to the left so badly. He has a nice jump and there is no reason for him to pursue this aggravating habit any longer. If he meets a jump with a wide spread, the left-handed bias will certainly make it

Figure 5.6 Hallelujah! The V poles work. Vanessa has held Gus's head firmly to the middle of the jump and he is doing well, but the slight curve of his body shows what he would prefer to do if given the chance.

a

b

Figures 5.7a and **b** It is vital for this eventer to go straight for the middle over the water jump.

wider and unnecessarily more difficult. The more Vanessa persists, the better he will jump. (Figures 5.7a and b)

Hard work on the grid is once again proven to get the required results (Figure 5.8)

Mary has the opposite problem with Maxi, he hangs to the right, but the method of encouraging him to jump better is the same (Figures 5.9, 5.10, 5.11 and 5.12).

Maxi is improving but he will still need some more practice with these exercises before he consistently jumps better (Figures 5.13a and b and 5.14). Patience and persistence with work on the stay-straight grid will produce the right result eventually (Figure 5.15).

right **Figure 5.8** Vanessa has so improved Gus with the grid that, at a show, he is lined up with the middle of the jump. She can comfortably look where she's going and trust him to stay straight.

Figure 5.9 Maxi has to jump much higher for not being in the middle.

Figure 5.10 The diagonal poles square him up to the middle of the crosses.

Figure 5.11 Mary has a job to steer Maxi straight even going in to this double. He's determined to hang to the right.

Figure 5.12 You can see here how Maxi is veering right across, almost to the wing, in spite of Mary's best efforts.

a

b

top row **Figures 5.13a** and **b** Mary and Maxi jump in quite well (a) but, even with the V poles keeping him straighter in the middle, Maxi still wants to cut off to the right as he jumps out (b).

above **Figure 5.14** Mary does her very best to keep maxi straight but the bias is still there.

right **Figure 5.15** On a show course, Maxi proves how all the serious work on the stay-straight grid has had an obvious effect.

6 The fan grid

The fan grid takes a bit of setting up, and you need to do it very accurately to get the most benefit from it (Diagram 7). It is, however, well worth the effort as it will help you to be much sharper and positive with the steering and control, and it will encourage your horse to be more responsive to how and where you want him to go. If your horse is finding the jumping work easy and starting to show a little arrogance, he may try to decide for himself which jump is next, and it may not be the one you want.

In a jump-off situation, you may want to turn while the horse wants to carry on over the original track. When you ask him to come round instead of carrying on to the jump he is convinced is next, he will be argumentative. The turn will be poor and he will still be thinking backwards to the jump he wanted to take instead of concentrating on the jump you intend to approach. Usually this is because the horse is keen; any jump will do for him, even if it is not in the right order and so this grid will help you give the right signals a little more quickly. Once he understands which jump you want, he will be fine, but if you don't tell him quickly enough, he will continue to set his sights on the jump he fancies and try to take charge. There is a choice of three jumps to go for and you must make your mind up which one *you* want and make sure he understands so that there is no confusion, no options.

Once you've jumped the straight grid, whichever option you choose next, 1, 2, or 3, you have two choices for your return jump before you head back down to the straight grid again. You can choose either a short turn or a wider turn, but if you don't let your horse know exactly what you want in time, he will find this exercise very confusing.

The grid can be as easy or as difficult as you wish to make it by altering the angles of jumps 1 and 3 and, as you improve, you will find that your jumping off turns and angles round a course of jumps will be much more effective. You will learn from the fan just how much you can ask on a turn and expect to receive, and you will also learn just how far you can go before your horse says 'I can't make it'.

Start off with a conventional 7-cross grid to warm up with and then change the grid so that you have two single crosses, a double cross and then the three jumps forming the fan effect on a four-stride distance 17.4–18.2 m (57–60 ft/19–20 yd) away from the double cross (Diagram 7). Work straight up the grid to jump number 2 of the fan to start with as a control exercise.

When you are going smoothly in a straight line, decide which route you are going to change to. Not only must you plan your route away from the straight grid, you need to decide which of the other two crosses you want to jump on your way back to the straight grid again (Figures 6.1a–f and 6.2a–f).

You must turn your head as you jump the double cross to look where you intend to go. Your horse has already got used to going straight on and so he

Diagram 7   The fan grid

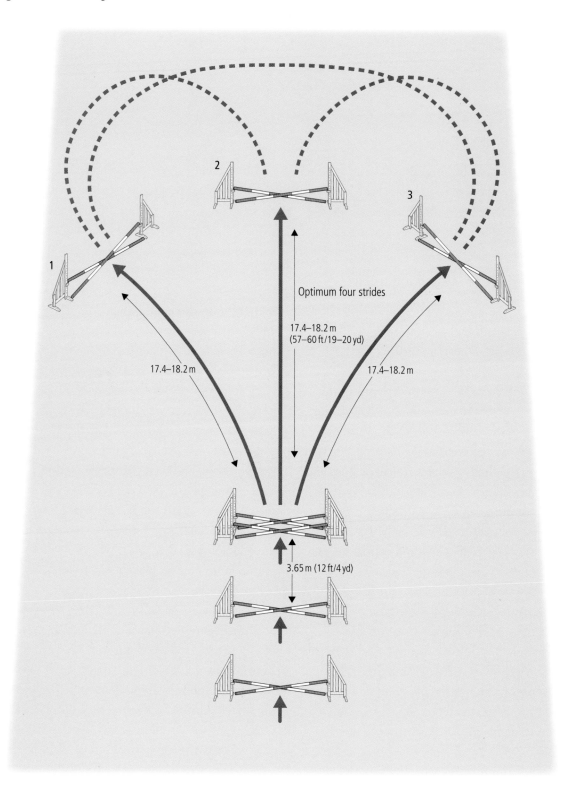

2

3

1

Optimum four strides

17.4–18.2 m
(57–60 ft/19–20 yd)

17.4–18.2 m

17.4–18.2 m

3.65 m (12 ft/4 yd)

Figures 6.1a–f Anna has decided to turn right to jump number 3. Dodo is well prepared and makes a lovely jump off four active strides.

won't be expecting a change of route, unless of course you tell him otherwise. Turning your head in the direction you want to go has two major effects on your jumping. Obviously the first is that you are actually looking where you mean to go, but the second more subtle effect is that your horse will pick up on your body language; the turning of your head brings about a subtle weight change and angling of the body that is his early warning system of what is to come and once he recognizes this he will be half prepared for the change of route. Don't expect him to cooperate immediately the first few times you use this grid, as he will remain fairly convinced that he is meant to carry on as before. Be ready to steer as you land and make sure you push your horse into the contact. The double cross poles are deliberately used to ask your horse to make a greater effort preceding the turn. You will then be able to practise everything: your timing, balance, rhythm, control, speed and steering all in the space of a couple of strides. If you get all these right, you will meet the crosses at either jump 1 or 3 perfectly. If you don't you will find the striding won't suit you as well as it did when you were in a straight line.

If you find that the double cross is throwing you too much out of balance to manage to produce everything quickly, change it to a single cross until you get the hang of it. Your horse won't make such a big effort and it will give you more time to sort out your timing and position. Remember, this isn't an exercise to jump bigger fences; it's primarily to improve your steering and control. Even if you work up to it gradually, the last jump in the line needs to give you the feel of an exaggerated jump so that you have to be sharp enough to be steady and steer, certainly by stride two, and preferably on stride one (Figures 6.3a–c).

A horse will always go better on the way back down the fan to the double cross as there is only one option to go for. The four strides are much

c

f

Figures 6.2a–f Looking in the direction she is going, Anna then takes a wide left turn to jump number 1 and back down the straight grid.

more consistent when the horse is focused on the jump. You must try very hard to get the last stride before the double cross as straight and square as possible so that the bounces are ridden as effectively 'out' as on the way 'in' to the exercise (Figure 6.4).

The fan is such a good grid for practising getting your steering right while still riding forwards. So many riders feel they have to check or slow down to look where they're going next instead of simply

a

b

d

e

looking further ahead. It is so easy to concentrate on the steering and to forget to keep up the impulsion which, even if your line is right, makes the jump difficult.

Once you have ridden the fan nicely, turning at the top end on both reins, start to vary your routes. If you change rein alternately, a clever horse will soon be quick enough to recognize what you intend and will start to anticipate. This know-all attitude is precisely what we are trying to put a stop to, so don't let it start to creep in. Do the grid two or three times the same way before you change and then maybe only once before changing back again.

There are so many alternatives you can employ to keep him listening to you; make sure you know where you intend to go, therefore, before you start the exercise. If you send him muddled signals because you have forgotten which route you mean to take you will only confuse him.

Try going straight up the middle to jump number 2, and then turn left or right back to 1 or 3. Or go across to number 1 or 3 and turn back over number 2 and straight down the middle to finish. These will obviously be much shorter turns, which can also be used to start to develop the balance, rhythm and outside rein support which will help

Figures 6.3a–c Siobhan has left it a little late to tell Asti where to go, but she persists and pushes and he gets it right, albeit with putting in an extra stride.

c

below **Figure 6.4** Abigail makes a super job of riding back down the fan.

b

a

you improve your jump-off routes and times. If you spin your horse on this 270 degree turn by leaning in and giving the outside rein away to help you steer, he will slant on the corner and any power from the inside hind leg will be lost. You will have a poor and unbalanced approach to the next jump. Think of keeping his head and neck vertical in front of you. Support with the outside rein while steering with the inside and look where you want to go. His neck shouldn't lean on the corner. If you drop your shoulder to indicate which direction you want, you will probably land on the wrong lead, and will be distracted all the way round the turn.

The loops or three-quarter circles at the top of the fan will help you recognize how tightly you can turn in a jump-off situation. If your helper counts the number of strides you take between fences, you will be able to have a very clear picture of how well you are doing. If you try to reduce the number of strides between jumps, then obviously your time round a turn should improve. Just make sure you don't try to turn so short that you have to check hard to do so, as this will take *more* time, not less. The turn must be smooth and flowing and if you

keep looking far enough ahead, your rhythm and power will make the approach to the next jump easy. And of course you still have the straight part of the grid to aim for.

When the steering and obedience are well established and your horse is letting you tell him where to go, you can always increase the size of the jumps 1, 2, and 3. Still leave them as uprights because you will want to jump them from both directions. If you change the angle of jumps 1 and 3 by setting the inside wing further away, the approach from, and the return to, the double cross can be made more difficult. If you change the angle the other way and move the outside wings away, the approach from and to the double cross will be easier, but the turn will be more of a U turn than a three-quarter circle. There are so many variations in this grid, and they are all good for both you and the horse. Remember that you must tell him clearly what you want in time for him to do as you ask. It will keep both of you on your toes.

Figures 6.5, 6.6a and b, 6.7a and b, 6.8, 6.9 and 6.10 show how the fan grid is such good preparation for jumping work both when practising and at shows.

Figure 6.5 After practising the fan grid, Abigail and Altro work on the practice course: they are both looking across from the narrow viaduct wall (jump number 6) to the parallel across the dogleg (jump number 7). She has prepared him well and he has responded.

above **Figures 6.6a** and **b** Altro flying over jumps at a show just as nicely as he did when going back over the double cross on the fan grid.

left **Figures 6.7a** and **b** Asti and Siobhan both know exactly where they're going next. On the practice course Siobhan is determined to ride positively on the related distance from the triple bar at number 3 to the planks at number 4.

Figure 6.8 Asti with his normal rider. Being a schoolmaster has done him no harm at all.

Figure 6.9 Anna is looking far enough ahead round the corner to the next jump and is ready to let Dodo know immediately where he's meant to go.

Figure 6.10 Shows present no problems for Dodo; he goes exactly where he's pointed.

7 The figure-of-eight grid exercises

A figure-of-eight grid gives you all the skills you need to practise and develop to help you negotiate a course of show jumps. You should already be proficient with doubles, combinations and related distances by working with straight grids, so now you need to sort out your steering and impulsion when you go round corners. And that's just to put you on the right path to jumping clear in the first round.

You will then be able to use these exercises to improve your jump-off times without hurrying and trying to go too fast. Turning, jumps on the angle and taking strides out are all made easier by practising in the right manner. It is no good galloping flat out in the jump-off and having poles down on the way; you might do the fastest time, but you will have the worst score. A far more subtle approach will be better. If you turn a little shorter, you will improve your time. If you start to learn how to jump on the angle, you will save a few strides when it matters most. Fewer strides round the course will obviously take less time, especially if you look far enough ahead so that you don't need to check the horse to see where you're going next.

As well as improving your jump-off skills, this grid should also sort out your canter leads and flying changes. So many riders fret and lose concentration round a course because their horse is on the wrong leg or disunited. They haven't the confidence to press on and allow the horse to sort his legs out. You should remember that the horse has been man- aging his own legs since the day he was born. Being disunited occasionally will not bother him in the slightest, he can soon correct that on the move, he doesn't have to come sedately back to trot and start off again. This grid will help you allow the horse to learn to do flying changes when you're on his back as well as he does them when galloping loose in his field. It will help him to land on the correct lead, sort out the disunited canter and generally improve the consistency and power of the canter all the way round a course and so improving the presentation and approach to the fence and the way he jumps.

Ben and Katharine, Jake and Suzy

Q *Ben won't change legs, the best he will do is change in front but not behind. How can I make him canter on the correct leg?*

Q *My new horse Jake has been fine on a straight grid, but he's sprawling on the corners when we jump a course. He also is having trouble with landing on the right leg. What's the solution?*

A *The figure-of-eight grid is all you need.*

Katharine wants Ben to cooperate and always corner on the correct lead but, when he is wrong, her tendency is to bring him back to trot and have another go. Suzy does the same with Jake; she doesn't like to pressurize him because they are just getting to know each other. Both riders need to recognize that they must give their horses a set of conditions and ride them in a balanced and positive way; the figure-of-eight grids are perfect for this. They must produce the right feel of inside leg to outside rein on landing and turning and allow Ben and Jake to work out for themselves that it is more comfortable to be in true canter.

Obviously the jumping will be better if you feel confident and happy because your horse is on the correct leg but is it such a disaster if he isn't? Certainly it is not so comfortable for you if he is disunited but as long as you deal confidently with the situation, the jumping will still be satisfactory. It is so easy to come back to trot when your horse's legs aren't behaving in canter as you would hope but if you are so protective, how will he ever learn to change the lead himself?

If you don't give him this opportunity to allow him to learn to sort his own legs out you will be restricted and distracted by the need to always be 'correct'. Don't be too sensitive and try to get the situation into perspective; if you are on the wrong leg and keep going, when you change the rein again you will be back on the correct lead.

A figure-of-eight grid is ideal for encouraging your horse to learn to change his lead and remain balanced. It is one of the first things I want my own young horses to learn, but I do my very best not to try to *teach* them. The figure-of-eight helps them to work out for themselves that flying changes or correcting the disunited canter is only what they would do in the field without a rider on. It is easier and more comfortable for them to have the correct lead, but it won't happen if you try to organize the change by leaning in and trying to indicate with your weight which leg you want him to lead on.

If you do lean in, your inside shoulder and hip will collapse slightly, your outside rein will soften, and you will actively encourage the wrong lead.

The figure-of-eight exercises

Diagram 8 shows all the variations of the figure-of-eight grid that will help with the problems discussed above.

Grid 1

Set up the grid as shown in Grid 1 with a four-stride distance between the two jumps. Build all the jumps with the sides of the poles raised to form fairly sharp X-shaped crosses. However bold or ambitious you may be with your steering, it is still a good idea to jump the fences in the middle, and the crosses will let you know how accurate you are. For fences 1 and 2 build double crosses, when you add fences 3 and 4, they should be just single crosses. If you are working in an arena, build 1 and 2 against the fence, if you are working in a field, use guide poles on each side of the jumps to stop you swinging wide.

Jump fences 1 and 2 straight several times making sure that you are riding consistently well and that your strides are strong and active. When your horse is warmed up, start the exercise. Ride towards fence 1 on the right rein, approaching on a diagonal line past fence 2. Aim for a point approximately 1.8 m (6 ft) in front of the fence and head for that point. The proximity of the fence or guiding poles will help to square you up on the last stride but do look far enough ahead to make sure that you jump the fence in the middle.

If you keep your shoulders level and do not ease your outside rein forward to help with the steering, you should land in an active and working canter, mostly with the correct lead. Don't worry if your

Diagram 8 Grid 1

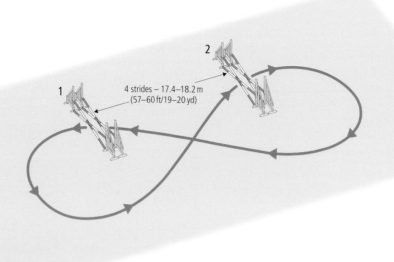

2

1

4 strides – 17.4–18.2 m
(57–60 ft/19–20 yd)

horse is on the wrong leg or disunited. Resist the urge to come back to trot, and concentrate instead on pushing him consistently into his supporting outside rein. He will either change or he won't, but the outside rein will keep him balanced if he is either disunited or isn't leading on the correct leg. Once you have landed, without 'motor biking' and leaning in, make a three-quarter turn to the left to prepare to head across on the diagonal to jump fence 2.

Stay in canter, whatever his legs are doing! Again, aim at a point 1.8 m (6 ft) in front of the fence to allow enough room on this angled approach to be able to square up on the take-off point for the jump. (Figures 7.1a–c.)

Figures 7.1a–c Suzy and Jake have been round this figure-of-eight two or three times, staying in canter the whole time, correct or incorrect! Jake is getting very cute. Although he has come across on the diagonal approach with left lead, as Suzy straightens him up on the last stride before fence 2 he does a very smart flying change ready to jump and land on his right leg; just what we were hoping for. Suzy has helped him do it easily as she has been balanced, held a very supportive outside rein and is looking where she means to go.

a

The angled approach will be made more or less difficult depending on the size of your three-quarter turn on the landing side of each jump. Try to keep the turn neat and fairly tight. If you drift too far out, the angle to the next jump will be more difficult. The fence or guiding poles will help you to square your approaches, but don't be too reliant on them. Practise steering as if they aren't there. Of course they will guide you and stop you overshooting, but as you work on this figure-of-eight, try to develop an independence and confidence in yourself to be able to point your horse where you want to go, regardless of ground poles or fence. When you jump a course, you will need to be able to look where you are going and steer independently, especially in a large outdoor arena. Carry on round your three-quarter turn to the right after fence number 2 and head back across to number 1 again, completing the figure-of-eight. Repeat the exercise!

As well as looking far enough ahead to practise your steering, don't forget how to ride over the jumps. Try to keep your weight level in the air, and don't allow yourself to anticipate the turn by collapsing or leaning your shoulder in. When you land,

support with your outside rein all the way round the turn. If you ease the outside rein forward to help you steer, you will lose power from the inside hind leg. If you drop your inside shoulder you will encourage the horse to lean in as he lands and actively encourage him to be either disunited or on the wrong lead. You need to have the right support and feel with the outside rein to hold him out plus enough action with your steering hand to turn him round the corner. As you come round the turn, don't let his head and neck be slanted in front of you.

Repeat this exercise four or five times on the figure-of-eight to try to establish some consistency and before you have a breather.

It would be nice if the turns and approaches were similar at each end. You should be thinking about taking around 16–18 strides between landing and taking off at the next jump. If one end is noticeably tighter or easier, check out how much you are doing with the outside rein. The more consistent the outside rein is, the more power you will produce on the turns and you won't be allowing him to lean in and be lazy with his inside hind leg. Then you can come round the turn tighter by actively steering

b

c

with your inside hand instead of just easing the outside hand forwards. He won't sprawl and you will get a much more consistent canter back across the new diagonal approach.

This may seem very obvious advice, but *do* practise looking where you mean to go. As soon as you land, turn your head and get your eye round the corner, looking across to the next jump. Don't ride round the turn, and then look for the next jump. It might not be where you expected it!

When you ride a whole course, your horse won't know where to go until you tell him. If you practise turning your head in plenty of time, he will pick up on your slight weight change. It will act as an early warning and indicate to him what you are going to ask.

When the exercise is repeated, obviously your horse is going to start to anticipate what you want, so make sure you don't allow him to lean into his turns.

Remember how you rode the end of the straight grids, telling him when to stay straight and asking him to turn, rather than allowing him to choose when.

If Katherine and Suzy work hard on this figure-of-eight grid in canter without getting uptight about the correct leading leg, they will give Ben and Jake the opportunity to learn to work out their legs for themselves. They must keep going in canter no matter what. Constantly coming back to trot to change must not be an option, their horses will never learn that it is simply easier to lead on the inside leg. Both girls must try hard to keep the inside shoulder up and not lean in, they must keep nagging with the inside leg into a very consistent outside rein and see what happens. It will work. It may not happen immediately, but if they persist in giving Ben and Jake the balance to allow them to change easily instead of trying too hard to organize them, they will get better and better.

Once you are quite happy with this exercise, ride it the opposite way.

Grid 2

The exercise shown in Grid 2 will give you slightly different options to practise. Again, start with fence 1 but this time approaching it on the right rein on the right circle. You should already be looking across the diagonal and planning how much angle you will need to take to be able to ride a balanced left-handed three-quarter turn for the approach to fence 2.

If you cut in too much, the three-quarter turn will be very tight, and if you go too wide, you will find it difficult to keep your rhythm and impulsion all the way. Try to follow more or less the line you rode on the earlier exercise, but it will be in reverse. It will give you a guide as to how much turn you can ask for without being over ambitious. You will find it more difficult on this route to stop your horse cutting in on the approach to the next fence and so you will have lots of opportunities to practise the use of the supporting outside rein and looking where you are going. Do remember to turn your head to look for the next fence, but keep your inside shoulder *up*.

A horse is going to try to lean in, not because he is being naughty, but because he is sure he knows where he is going, and is keen to get there. He doesn't recognize that it will be easier to jump if he allows his rider to hold and support him by his outside rein so that his hind leg remains active underneath him.

You have already practised *not* leaning in on the other grids, so don't treat this grid any differently.

As with the first figure-of-eight exercise, repeat this one four or five times before you have a breather. Stay in canter all the way round regardless of which leg your horse is leading with. You should

Diagram 8 Grid 2

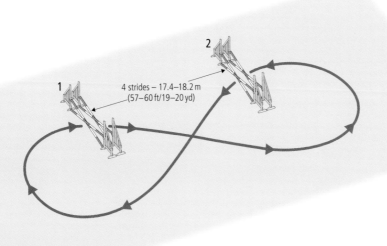

find if you remain consistent in your riding and don't let him lean in on the turns, more and more often you will land on the correct leg. If you land on the 'wrong' lead and keep going, the flying changes will start to happen. Just keep going and let him learn. The exercise will become easier and more effective the more you do it. (Figures 7.2a–c)

Grid 3

When you feel happy and confident with Grid 2, it is time to build Grid 3 by adding two more fences, 3 and 4 in the positions shown. Get your tape out again and measure a five-stride distance from the middle of fence 3 to the middle of 2, and from the middle of fence 4 to the middle of 1.

Approaching on the left rein between fences 2 and 4, start the grid at fence 1, and then practise your steering, rhythm and impulsion round the half circle to enable you to jump fence 3 square on. You want to be looking across to fence 2 so that the line between them is more or less direct and straight. Remember, you are aiming for a point slightly in

front of fence 2 to enable you to have room to square up to the fence from that diagonal approach to the jump. Once you've jumped 2, land and work hard round the three-quarter turn to 4. The quicker you balance up after the jumps and push into your supporting outside rein, the sooner you will be able to establish the impulsion which will make it easy for your horse to turn and keep jumping.

Certainly the fence or the guiding poles on the ground will help you, but try very hard not to rely on them. If you are looking far enough ahead, the route should be straightforward. And if you find it too difficult to start with, give yourself a bit more room on the three-quarter turn; it will give you more time to practise looking where you mean to go.

Try to stay in canter and repeat the exercise four or five times until you feel confident about maintaining a similar strong impulsion all the way round. This is where you will discover how vital it is to look far enough ahead while keeping up the rhythm. Your horse should be landing more and more consistently on the correct lead, and if he doesn't, keep going. Let him learn; just make sure

b

a

c

Figures 7.2a–c Katherine and Ben make a nice active jump over number 1 and he goes across the diagonal in right canter. Katherine stays level and holds him out on the turn; he recognizes the change of direction and does a perfect flying change on the corner. There is no loss of rhythm and power, he does a strong and accurate jump over number 2 and is about to land in true left canter ready for the opposite diagonal line across the arena.

Diagram 8 Grid 3

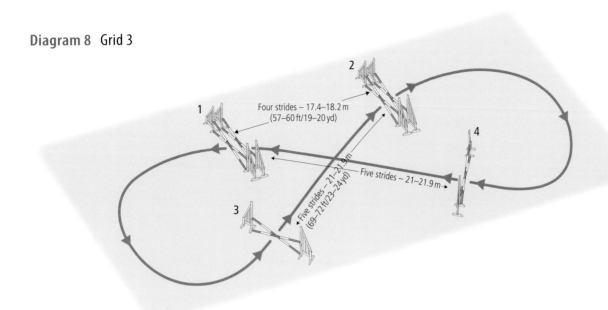

that your body is level, your inside shoulder is up and you have enough feel on the outside rein to stop him slanting in. Your steering should be accurate enough to present him square on and in the middle to all the fences, and will give you the chance to practise maintaining a strong canter and steering at the same time. It is totally unnecessary to check your horse to give yourself more time to look to see where you want to go! (Figures 7.3a–d.)

When you feel confident with this exercise, start to reduce the number of strides you take round the turn at each end; it is a great exercise for practising jump offs. You won't be able to take out strides across the diagonal approaches because you need to keep in a rhythm and the distance should be a measured five strides. If you try to zoom across on four to save time, your horse will go fast and flat, you won't be as accurate with the next jump, and he will be too fast after either fence 1 or 2 to do a nice short three-quarter turn back to 3 or 4. Don't try to improve dramatically immediately, one fewer stride is a good start, and then try to gradually reduce the number of

strides each time you ride the grid. Again, you will soon discover how much you can ask for and receive, or not! If you overdo it and try to turn too ambitiously, you simply won't make it. At best you will knock poles down, at worst you will run out. If you get too keen, your horse will get flustered. Try to reduce the number of strides sensibly without hurrying so that your horse is not even aware that you want to get round the corners more quickly.

Grid 4

Repeat the above exercise in the opposite direction, starting with fence number 1 off the right rein. Riding the grid this way round will give you the chance to start practising jumping slightly on the angle. You can see from the diagram that if you steer fractionally wider as you approach fences 1 or 2 and jump them just a little bit across on the angle you will be able to look for more of a straight line across the diagonal to jumps 3 and 4, rather than landing and turning more acutely to get the

a

b

c

d

Figures 7.3a–d Ben has jumped fence number 3 nicely off left canter; Katherine has stayed very level and looked across to number 2. Ben has picked up her intentions, landed nicely on the right lead and powered across to number 2 and jumped it well, landing in the correct lead for the next turn. Katherine has landed well in balance and is already pushing Ben into her outside rein. She is looking where she wants to go and rides economically round the corner without having to check.

Diagram 8   Grid 4

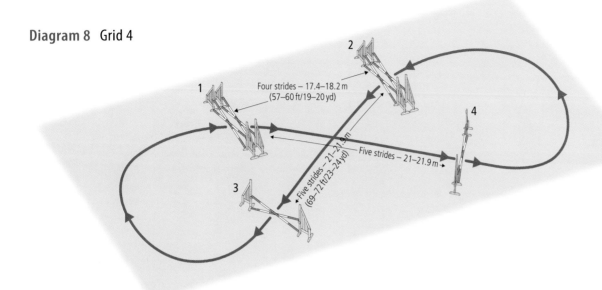

Four strides – 17.4–18.2 m
(57–60 ft/19–20 yd)

Five strides – 21–21.9 m
(69–72 ft/23–24 yd)

Five strides – 21–21.9 m

approach square (Figures 7.4a and b). The fence or boundary poles will stop you going too wide on the turns to 1 and 2 and will also help square you up to the jumps if you have been a little ambitious in turning on your half circles. If you ride all the turns with lots of leg into a strong and consistent outside rein, you will have every opportunity to cut the number of strides round the corners to the next jumps. Don't be so keen that you are almost bouncing off the fence to get in line for jumps 1 and 2, use the fence to help you recognize just how easily your horse will get round the corner if you are consistent and positive with the steering. You need to be able to ride the same sort of turns in a jump-off without a fence alongside to help you.

Your timing over the jumps is vital, and something you can practise every time you ride the grid. Because by now you should be happier with the canter, don't be in too much of a hurry to land to get on with your turn. If you anticipate your landing, especially when you are eager to get to the next jump, you might shift your weight and cause the landing to happen a little too soon. As soon as

your horse feels you change your balance preparing to land, he will be encouraged to get his undercarriage down too, and sometimes it will be too early making him rattle the pole behind. However keen you are to improve your time and to take more strides out, if you anticipate the landing yourself and come down a bit too quickly you will take poles with you. Get your timing right. You need to hover a bit longer in the air than you think to give your horse time to complete the jump accurately. If he feels you bustling him along, it will make him hurry and more likely to knock poles. And once you've completed the turn, don't just sit there and think how well you've done with your presentation and approach to the next jump. If you relax a little because your steering has gone well and if you don't keep nudging off the turn and all the way to the next jump, he will fade underneath you and you will lose your power. It isn't enough to just push round a sharp turn; you must keep pushing strongly as you straighten up, all the way to the jump, without easing up.

To get the most out of this exercise just make

a

b

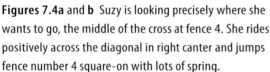

Figures 7.4a and **b** Suzy is looking precisely where she wants to go, the middle of the cross at fence 4. She rides positively across the diagonal in right canter and jumps fence number 4 square-on with lots of spring.

sure you ride all the turns with a strong outside rein and insist that your horse *does not* lean in.

You will find that, as you progress with all the exercises, the canter leads will be improving. The extra fences, 3 and 4, will really help your horse to land in true canter and if at first it doesn't work, just keep going and allow things to improve, don't try to force the improvement to happen. Remember, you must allow your horse to recognize for himself that it is easier to be on the right leg.

You can see from the diagrams of Grids 3 and 4

that the degree of difficulty of the grid may be varied by the alteration of the angle of these jumps. As you become more proficient, alter the angles but only very slightly and, again, practise riding a more acute angle or a wider circle, whichever you feel needs a little more attention and practice. It is a grid you can adapt easily to produce the sort of improvement you need at the time, i.e. it is tailor-made for you to play with and can be kinder or more severe to suit whatever standard of horse you are riding. You can, for example, make the jumps into parallels and uprights with horizontal poles instead of crosses; there's no limit to how much you can test yourself and your horse, but increase the difficulty gradually. As with all the grids recommended, if things go wrong it is so simple to backtrack a step to build up confidence again.

When you are happy with this work, a slight alteration to the distances will give you the chance to practise riding dogleg approaches.

Grids 5 and 6

With Grid 5, start off with jump number 1 approaching it on a left rein between jumps 2 and 4 and then follow the route on the diagram.

For Grid 6, start off with jump number 1 approaching it from the right rein.

The routes to be practised are similar to the first four exercises, but the distances give you more room to ride a dogleg approach. You should be position-ing the fences to allow six or seven strides between fences 1 and 4, or 2 and 3, depending on which route you choose. Use the tape but do pace the distances on the diagonals between the fences on your own feet. Try to decide where you should aim for on the approach across the diagonal which will give you the most beneficial stride. The grid-work distance and related distance table on page 25 will help you plan your route and you should try to ride it so that you have at least one or, better still, two straight strides on the take-off side of all the fences. If you ride the diagonal on a curve instead of a posi-tive and accurate dogleg you will probably let the horse lean in and arrive at the next jump crooked

Diagram 8 Grids 5 and 6

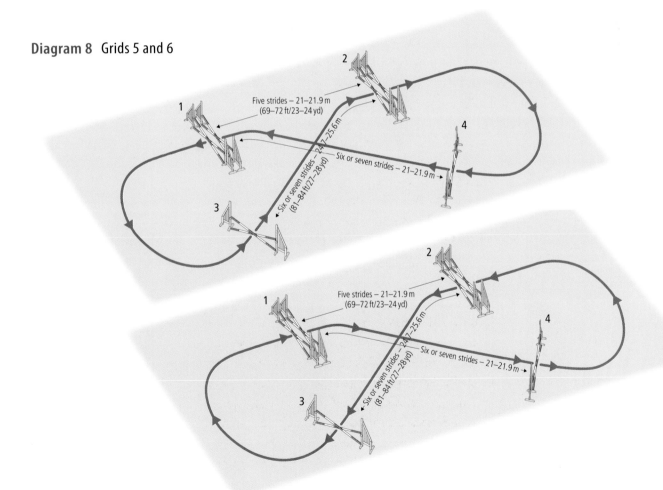

Five strides – 21–21.9 m
(69–72 ft/23–24 yd)

Six or seven strides – 24.1–25.6 m
(81–84 ft/27–28 yd)

Six or seven strides – 21–21.9 m

Suitable for practising dogleg approaches. At this longer distance between the jumps, the number of strides taken depends on the route you take across the dogleg. If you cut in it will be fewer strides, a short six, than if you go a little wider, a longer seven.

without enough impulsion, resulting in a poor landing and getaway. Unless you straighten up to the fence the curved approach will throw you off in the wrong direction when you land. If you are practising your jump-offs, you might save a stride on the curved approach, but you will take two strides further *after* the jump to get back on track again. It won't do much for your canter leads either.

Look far enough ahead on both routes so that you are jumping all four jumps in the middle and remember, *no* checking and slowing down to give you extra time to see where you are going to go. Inside leg pushing to outside rein support will be the key to success on all your turns, so keep up the consistency of your riding. Both you and your horse will enjoy the jumping so much more, and do it better.

After practising in the arena, Suzy and Katherine had a go round the practice course.

The work she did on this grid has really helped Susie and they stayed in true canter all the way round (Figure 7.5).

This grid had the same effect on Ben's canter (Figure 7.6).

When you are practising this grid at home, don't give up too easily.

You may need to repeat all these figure-of-eight exercises over a few sessions before you see significant improvement, or you may find that your horse gets the knack of the true canter very quickly. One thing is for sure, your jump-off skills will improve rapidly.

If you're short of jump material, poles placed on the ground where the four jumps are set will still help you produce the flying changes that will improve your course jumping a great deal. If your horse doesn't change leads, by the time you come round the next turn he will once again be on the

below left **Figure 7.5** Suzy has turned her head right to look where she's going next, round the corner to number 6, but held a very supportive left rein. Jake is straight over the jump and about to land and get away in a nice strong right canter.

below right **Figure 7.6** Katherine and Ben are totally focused and there is no question about the commitment to ride an accurate dogleg approach from the narrow jump at 6 to the parallel at 7.

correct lead. If you stay very relaxed in your attitude, remain patient and repeat the work consistently, rather than trying to force the issue, it will work eventually; the only question will be how many times you have to repeat it.

There is one other exercise you should do after doing all this twisting and turning: you have to make sure that your horse will still go in a straight line. However hard you try to encourage the horse to listen to you, it will be almost impossible to avoid him anticipating his turns, so to finish this particular work, always ride a straight line again over fences 1 and 2. It simply ensures that the horse is genuinely listening to you; make sure, therefore, that you tell him clearly what you want. *Look* along a straight line and remember how you worked hard on a straight grid to keep him active and accurate.

With only four jumps, you can practise nearly all the skills you need to jump a full course proficiently. Every problem a course builder can throw at you

as far as the track is concerned can be practised with the judicious use of grids. When you need to practise for jump-off situations, the turns and angles on this type of grid make it ideal to teach you to be proficient in all the skills required to help you do well at shows. The only thing you need to do next is put these exercises into practice round a course of jumps.

If you have no opportunity to practise over a full course, the addition of one extra jump to the figure-of-eight fences will give you the chance to ride a longer exercise of nine or ten efforts consecutively.

The five-fence course plan

You can see from the suggested route on this five-fence course that you need to be very positive to ensure the horse knows where he is going next. Because you have already worked extensively round the figure-of-eight exercises he will be pretty certain

Diagram 8   Five-fence course plan

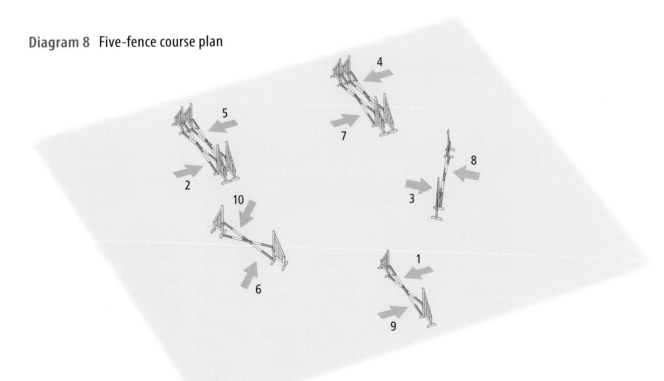

to anticipate where he is going at first and so unless you tell him clearly and in plenty of time, he will hesitate when you change his route and you will lose your rhythm. It will do you both good to have a change of route and will reinforce that you are in charge of the steering.

Try very hard not to check and slow down to see where you are going next. If you forget the planned route, he won't know, just jump anything, but jump it well. All five jumps can be jumped from either direction, and there are endless possibilities; just make sure you tell the horse in time so that there are no misunderstandings (Figure 7.7).

Once again, putting in the time and effort on the grid has helped these partnerships reap the rewards at shows (Figures 7.8, 7.9 and 7.10).

Figure 7.7 Ben might have been surprised to see another jump but Katherine has given him no option but to jump it in the middle.

Figure 7.8 The figure-of-eight grid has encouraged Suzy to be very positive with Jake in the jump off, and she has produced a strong stride from him through the double, making the jump out very easy.

above **Figure 7.9** A very accurate line on a dogleg approach.

above right **Figure 7.10** All that hard work on the grid has helped Suzy and Jake come off the corner strongly and have time and room for a good presentation and approach to this spooky jump.

8 Jumping passenger or jumping partner?

> **Q** *My new horse was perfect when I bought him. Now he's stopping, running out or charging off with me. Why is he doing it?*
>
> **A** *Because he can; you have become a passenger.*

When you plan to jump, if your horse pleases himself and not you, you are definitely a passenger, and you need to do something about it quickly before he pleases himself more and you less. If you ask him clearly to cooperate with your wishes he should say 'yes'; if he says 'no' or 'maybe' you have some way to go towards establishing the right balance of power (Figure 8.1).

You will soon discover what sort of relationship you have with your horse if you analyse how willing and cooperative he is to comply with your wishes. If you are a passenger, then he will make all the major decisions and will decide for himself whether he will do as you ask or not. If he is keen to do what you want, it will be on his terms because it suits him to cooperate. A horse that enjoys jumping will do as you ask quite nicely until he decides he doesn't want to behave any more, and then you will find out who has the initiative. He will work on autopilot for a bit, taking you along with him, but if things go wrong or he gets fed up he won't be willing to put in some extra effort to help you out. He will soon realize that you have been too easy going and

allowed little bad habits to develop that you haven't recognized. He will, therefore, pick and choose when to behave well or not, and this attitude is accentuated when jumping is on the agenda.

However well a horse has been going, once he decides he has done enough, you will have an argument on your hands, an argument that has been brewing all the time you haven't been quite assertive enough. However delighted you are with your lovely new horse, you must remember you have bought him to please you, not the other way round. Any instructions you give him should be very clear. Even if you are sure he is going to jump nicely without much effort from you, don't neglect to make that effort. If you assume that all is well and he will automatically keep doing the job because he enjoys it, you will be very much mistaken. Horses can be so cheeky and take you by surprise with their naughty behaviour, but usually the warning signs have been there. If you have not been quick enough to recognize them, you deserve to be labelled a 'passenger'.

Try to look at the degree of being in control in percentage ratios. Obviously the perfect partnership is 50/50, but this is very hard to achieve and maintain as you and the new horse get to know each other, especially when jumping.

If you are only 35 or 40 per cent in charge, you can be considered to be a passenger; you are riding the horse but not necessarily in control. If the horse wants to take the initiative, he will be able to do so without a great deal of argument from the rider (Figure 8.2).

As you gain the confidence to be more assertive, the balance will shift and you will become more of a partner, taking your degree of control up above the 40/60 ratio currently in his favour, and then gradually improving until the partnership is more equal at 50/50. The horse will be required to do as you ask not to do just as he pleases. To be the senior partner with control of the proceedings, an ideal balance would be 51/49 in your favour with you making the decisions and the horse cooperating willingly.

If the horse decides not to behave as you wish, then you must recognize that sometimes you must gear yourself up to be far more assertive to counteract this attitude (Figure 8.3). Once you have been positive enough to gain the initiative and your horse starts to listen to you, you can level off the balance of power to foster, and hopefully maintain, a spirit of friendly cooperation, a partnership. If the partnership is unequal, make sure it is in your favour.

above **Figure 8.1** Is that a 'no' or a 'maybe'? Cahan is telling Zena what's what here.

Figure 8.2 Leo is keen to jump, which is admirable, but he has ignored Jo's wishes to steady across the related distance from jump 3 to 4. He has taken a stride out and hurdled the planks; 60/40 to Leo!

Figure 8.3 Jo is bossier, Leo is more accepting, and it looks like 51/49 to Jo.

The top riders seem to be able to have a totally equal partnership with their horses, but this comes with years of practice and expertise from the rider and it is why they are top riders. They have an instinctive knowledge of how to produce the best reaction from the horse. There is an almost psychic link between them, with no misunderstandings, particularly when they are jumping. The well-schooled horse is encouraged to do his best without the rider being too domineering; horse and rider are in harmony. It would be difficult to keep forcing a horse to jump well enough to win over big fences, even if he is very talented.

A working partnership has to be established. A horse that is not enjoying his work, however strongly ridden, will be perhaps in the percentage range of 80/20 rider dominance. The horse will always be on the lookout for the rider's attitude to soften slightly and, if he gets the chance to be evasive, he will take that opportunity in a flash. You don't want your new horse to get to that stage; you don't want to be on guard all the time. If you aren't compatible he might as well go.

Fortunately, with a little attention to detail, this should not have to happen because any major disagreements should be avoidable. Presumably you have acquired the horse because he fits the bill and is exactly what you wanted, and there is usually a honeymoon period when the horse is insecure in new surroundings and tries to please you. But it won't take him too long to get his hooves under the table, especially if you are going out of your way to try to make him like you! If your new horse is always trying to be the boss, you must understand that he will take every opportunity to achieve what he thinks is a victory over you, especially when jumping. There are so many more opportunities to be out of balance and insecure when you leave the ground and you don't want the unexpected happening because you don't understand what has gone wrong.

The balance of power will fluctuate in different situations: very often you will be glad for the horse to take the initiative, sometimes you will need to have more input to help the horse out but, if you can achieve a happy mutual understanding, you and the horse should be able to help each other. But do try for consistency.

If you slip back into being a passenger again, the horse will recognize this lapse immediately and is likely to assume at least a 60/40 control. He will either try to dictate the speed and steering in a far more aggressive manner, or he will become evasive and nappy, or, unfortunately, both. Even if your initial performances have been good, your jumping will rapidly deteriorate in direct ratio to the degree you are a passenger.

A satisfactory partnership will only be formed when a horse and rider want to do the same things in harmony. If you try to get the horse to do what you want without success, you will stay a passenger and the horse will remain the boss.

Zac and **Reiko**

Q *I'm an inexperienced rider with a new horse. How can I form a good partnership when we start jumping?*

A *You need to learn not to be a passenger, to get to know your horse over the jumps and to build up your understanding, confidence and experience.*

Reiko wants to establish a partnership, not be a passenger. She has only recently started jumping, and is very keen to improve as quickly as possible. She had been to a few low-key shows with her previous horse who has now retired, and wants to make the most of her new partnership with Zac.

She had not jumped him before this training session and so the obvious way to get to know him was to jump as many jumps as possible in order to get the right sort of feeling both for the horse and jumping, and also to learn which buttons to push to get the best response. Any partnership with your horse is dictated by your experience and confidence, and your horse's willingness to cooperate with you.

A novice rider will be a passenger until they have gained enough experience to start to ask the horse to do as they wish instead of allowing him to do what he wants. When you have a nice horse who likes to be cooperative, he is unlikely to try to thwart what the rider wants to do. Most horses prefer the easy life, and as long as they find the work straightforward they will do their best.

Zac looks great and as long as he understands what the rider wants, he can't see any point in arguing (Figures 8.4a and b). He just gets on with

Figures 8.4a and b Zac looks very keen and happy down this long grid with 7 crosses. By the time Reiko gets to the end, she manages to level them both up. You can see Zac is going a little too fast as he 'plaits' a foreleg to miss the pole.

a

b

it because he likes what he's doing. It isn't hard for him to go through this grid consistently as he has plenty of enthusiasm. He is ideal for Reiko to gain some experience with and develop her skills without worrying too much about keeping the horse going forward. He may be in charge of the relationship at the moment, but you can see he has no inclination to be difficult as he is having fun.

It is my job to look out for trouble brewing so that it can be avoided, and I'm just slightly concerned about Zac's speed. Obviously he knows what he is doing and is very confident and competent, but Reiko's inclination to be a little too forward encourages him to be even faster (Figure 8.5).

Once Reiko has enough confidence to deal with this, she will be well on her way to becoming a partner. It takes a bit of time to get the confidence to try to take charge as, naturally, she will be slightly unsure that she is doing the right things. But she must let him know that she wants a steadier speed otherwise he will go faster and faster (Figure 8.6). If Reiko keeps her leg on when she asks Zac to steady,

there will be no misunderstandings. If she just checks him without using any leg, he will wonder why she wants to pull him up in the middle of the grid.

It is always daunting for an inexperienced rider to start with a new horse, and practising with this sort of grid on a genuine horse who knows what he is doing is ideal. Reiko can concentrate on allowing the correct and comfortable position to develop, rather than having to worry about making life easy for the novice horse. It is by far the best exercise I know to help the less-experienced rider feel, and allow the development of, the jumping position, and to realize just how little they need to arrange themselves in what they think is the 'correct' position. Once the complete beginner gains a little more expertise they can begin to 'see a stride' and anticipate the take-off point, which encourages them to exaggerate going forwards over the horse's shoulder as they try to do better. If they aren't perfectly balanced, they may push the hands forward, usually in an effort to avoid catching the horse in the mouth as he jumps.

Figure 8.5 Reiko tries hard to look up and not let Zac pull her forward. It is a perfect grid to develop the right balance between leg and hand. But he doesn't have to accelerate through the grid and even at this early stage Reiko must take a bit more charge and ask him to steady. Just notice how clever Zac is: he is traveling a bit fast and slightly to his left and has also 'plaited' his left fore again.

above left **Figure 8.6** Zac is getting keen and although Reiko is looking up nicely, he is just pulling her too far forward over his shoulder: 60/40 to Zac.

above right **Figure 8.7** Reiko is much more secure here. She has steadied Zac, her lower leg is in a more secure position, and her shoulders are just over Zac's withers instead of above his neck: 51/49 to Reiko.

Nearly everyone who wants to jump is aware of the theory about allowing the horse to stretch and round over the fence, which is admirable, but you won't encourage him to jump well if you throw the reins up his neck and round his ears. Just when your horse needs the supporting contact most, on the take-off point, it is suddenly thrown away, letting all the impulsion generated from the leg dissipate immediately.

It is irresistible and understandable to try to imitate the top riders, but you should notice that their contact is always consistent on the approach, takeoff, over the fence, and when landing. They wait for a horse to come up in front of them, support him with the contact and fold into balance as the horse comes up, not before he leaves the ground. If you try to achieve this position by arranging yourself into what you think is 'the jumping position' too soon before the fence, the less effective you will be. It will certainly make it more difficult for the horse to jump successfully as he will be asked to operate with all his impulsion lost at the last second.

To prevent this happening, try the following, and try it every time you jump until you no longer need to think too hard about it. As you approach the grid, ease your seat slightly off the saddle and allow all your weight to drop down into the stirrups through your hip, knee and ankle joints. You should still find it easy to encourage your horse forward from your leg. Let your position 'float' a little. If you keep your chin up and try hard not to look down, it will stop you being too far forwards over the horse's shoulder. Try very hard to keep a consistent contact with the reins that is not too strong but very supportive. Your hands will allow more than enough 'give' as the balance of your body absorbs the movement of the horse and you won't need to shoot them forwards at each effort.

The very nature of the grid exercise will mean

that as you balance with your weight in the stirrups, the movement of the horse should feel like a slightly exaggerated canter. Aim to have the same supportive feel on the reins all the way through the grid, so that you finish the grid and canter away with the same feeling you had as when you approached.

It is the consistency of the feel that you need to try so hard to achieve, not a change in style as you are about to take off. If you can get this feeling by sheer repetition rather than too much theory, you are well on the way to finding the ideal position for you.

Obviously the longer grid will give you more opportunities to find that comfortable working position, but if you do not have enough material for 6 or 7 crosses, 2 or 3 is better than none. Don't skimp on this work, it will help you form the basis of your future partnership (Figures 8.8, 8.9a and b, 8.10 and 8.11).

Figure 8.8 When the grid was made into a small combination with low cross poles in between, Zac and Reiko start to work in harmony. Reiko's weight is in the stirrup, there is a slight float to the seat, a consistent contact and she is looking up: the ideal prescription for forming a partnership.

Figures 8.9a and **b** The partnership continues to improve as Reiko develops enough confidence to be a little more positive with controlling the speed.

a

b

It has been a valuable first session for Reiko and Zac. Reiko has realized that however much Zac wants to push on and jump and however much she is enjoying the grid work, she must be the steadying influence and be in charge; a partner with a say in the proceedings, not a passenger to be taken advantage of. Zac would soon become unruly if allowed to please himself entirely, and so the basis of their future jumping relationship needs to be established straightaway. The grid is the perfect place to set the boundaries of his future behaviour.

Figure 8.10 Thanks to the progressive and repetitive combination grid, Reiko and Zac are soon jumping a nice fence as equal partners.

Figure 8.11 Reiko is concentrating very hard at her first show with Zac.

9 The value of canter poles

Canter poles, *not* placing poles, can help a variety of horses and ponies to improve their striding and power, and so improve the way they cope with their jumps. They must be used with the right attitude: viewed as an aid to let the rider know if they are doing well enough in the canter to get the best out of their horses rather than as a hazard or nuisance to be endured. Canter poles encourage consistency, energy and impulsion. If they are set correctly they will highlight clearly any areas in which the rider should be trying to do better, and once the principles of using them for improving jumping are understood, they are an invaluable aid for someone working alone or without experienced advice.

With half a dozen poles you can do so much to improve the way you produce the up-tempo or 'up' jumping canter required to do your best when jumping. The poles will tell you *immediately* if your canter is too fast, too slow, too short, too long, too lazy, or too bouncy. You should be able to recognize everything a trainer might pull you up on. While you are riding try to analyse just how your horse is popping over the poles. Is he falling shorter as he goes through them and having to stretch at the end? Is he gaining too much ground? Are the poles in the same place with each stride? If he has a foreleg each side of the pole, have you the confidence to keep riding *in exactly the same way* so that he has a foreleg each side of every pole in the line?

Flying changes can also be developed if the canter poles are placed on the ground in the same position as the jumps in the figure-of-eight grid (see Chapter 7) and the work is carried out over the same routes. If your horse adopts too casual a manner in his work, you can use the canter poles in the same way as Shelly did for CJ in the Could Do Better chapter (see page 180).

Just make sure you measure the distances correctly and try to have someone with you to reinstate the poles if you kick them out of position on the way through, because you'll soon get fed up if you have to keep getting off to re-set them. You will only want help for a few minutes as both you and the horse will soon get fed up with the repetition, and if you start to get sloppy over them all the benefit of the previous work will be lost. Little and often is better anyway. You can vary the work by removing an odd pole here and there to see if you can keep up the canter consistently when there is a gap.

There are so many different types, shapes and sizes of horses, but they will all jump better for using something as plain and simple as canter poles, as long as you recognize they are an aid to tell you if you are working well enough. Don't rely on the poles to do all the work for you. Sharpen up with the timing of your aids. If you are trying to lengthen, don't just go faster and think you're doing well. Keep looking up and don't throw your hands forward in an attempt to increase the length of stride, only your legs will do that. If you need to shorten the stride, sharpen up your reactions to gather your horse underneath you all the way through the grid to keep him in the bouncy canter you need to jump well rather than the slightly long and sprawled canter he might prefer.

Whatever you need to do, do it quickly and clearly and keep it up through the whole exercise and beyond. If you let the horse 'collapse' as soon as the poles are finished, you haven't understood what the work is all about.

Canter-pole work is designed to help you *know* when your canter is good enough for better jumping; you are not doing it just to do fairly well for the duration of the poles. You will know you are working well enough when the canter before, through, and after the poles feels exactly the same; that's what you should be aiming for. If you can manage six good strides, with a bit of application and hard work you should be able to get the same feeling over thirty strides, or as many as it will take to go round a course, without needing thirty plus poles.

Even when you're doing well with your jumping, check yourself occasionally with the poles to make sure the canter isn't deteriorating slightly without you being aware of it. It is such an easy exercise to set up, so there are no excuses not to do it!

10 Canter poles and the lazy novice

Shamrock and Tory

Q *Why does Shamrock keep putting extra strides in?*

A *He's just not working hard enough.*

Shamrock is a nice young horse who has been brought on very carefully over the last year. He has done his conventional grid work and is really ready to work a bit harder and stop being such a baby. He is very familiar with the grid and canter poles, but he can't help being a ninny going down them the first time (Figure 10.1).

However much leg Tory gives him, Shamrock always goes very greenly over the grid the first time. Because he has been rather immature, he has been given every chance to build up his jumping grid work very gradually and carefully, and he still thinks he is a baby because he has been brought on so sympathetically. (Figure 10.2 and Diagram 9)

It really is time for him to grow up and work a bit harder. He most certainly is not going to be overfaced by being asked to jump bigger grids and courses, but Tory is about to ask him to shape up a bit and do as he is asked more effectively the first time instead of after a succession of dress rehearsals.

All he needs to do is work harder from Tory's leg,

Figure 10.1 This isn't the first time Shamrock has done his grid work, although you might think it is!

without it wearing her out to make him move. It is getting to the stage when it is exasperating for her, as on the few occasions when he fires up, he is a delight to ride, bold and accurate with his jumping instead of bumbling over and just getting by. If only she can make him *work harder*, not jump bigger or wider, the jumping will be much easier for him too. He doesn't need to be smacked to make him jump, but he does need to understand that a half-hearted response to her encouragement is not enough.

Figure 10.2 Shamrock's grid is very straightforward with three canter poles in to a small jump with three canter poles away. There are guide poles on each side to help him stay straight.

Diagram 9 Shamrock's grid

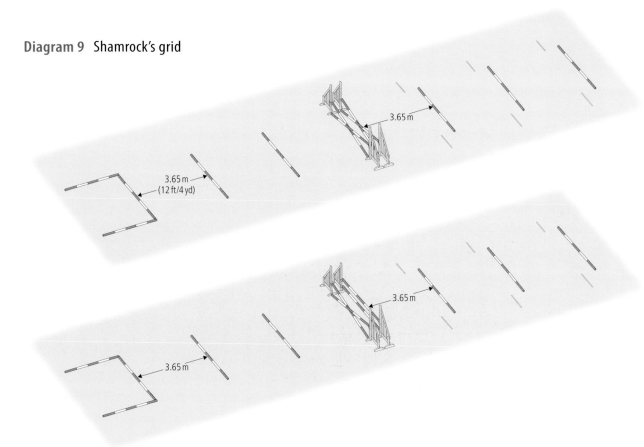

Don't forget that when you use double wings in the middle of the grid, the canter poles out must still be measured carefully to 3.65 m.

Tory knows he is being lazy, and by using the canter poles placed before and after the grid, she can recognize just how idle he is when he has jumped (Figures 10.3a and b). You can see how he is not making up anywhere near enough ground to have those poles in the same place for each of his canter strides. He falls backwards more at each one. Shamrock either has to stretch or make a blunder as he really doesn't operate strongly from his back end. All he does is negotiate them half-heartedly because he is lazy and can't see the need to operate properly over a few poles on the floor. But these few poles on the floor are letting Tory physically feel and recognize just how lacking in strength the canter is.

If we don't use the poles I can tell her that the canter away isn't good enough, and I know she believes me, but the poles on the ground give her incontrovertible proof that he is not doing well enough. After the middle jump, when he has one front leg one side of the canter pole and the second front leg the other side, it cannot fail to convince her totally that he must do better. If he won't work hard enough to do what she wants over a few poles on the floor, something has to change! And Tory is the one to make the change. He won't volunteer to work harder because she wishes it; he's quite happy drifting along doing his own thing, working at only about 60 per cent of his full capacity. It simply isn't good enough and Tory needs to look at the way she warms him up for jumping.

Because he is young and sweet and Tory is kind, he has been rather mollycoddled and not pressed to work quite hard enough to produce enough impulsion to make the jumping job easy. He is going to event, and now he is going out and about to shows to further his education. It is disappointing when he puts in bunny hops when show jumping, purely because his canter isn't strong and lively enough. The cross-country jumping is mostly satisfactory as he enjoys that and, of course, he has a lot more time between each jumping effort; the work isn't so concentrated and Tory can get him to bowl along in a nice rhythm, although he still can be sticky at some of the jumps and pop his extra stride in. That stride is not necessary and it is almost as if he doesn't want to exert himself and put in *too* much effort; he

a

b

Figures 10.3a and b In spite of all Tory's encouragement, you can see that Shamrock is not working hard enough. He certainly shouldn't have one foot each side of the pole. Tory has to repeat this several times until she gets him motivated.

simply gets by! But not any longer, the kid gloves are off, and Tory is going to insist that he *works*.

When you start to warm up the lazy horse, don't use flat work or dressage. Tory can make him look very nice on the flat, but he really isn't making the effort to come through enough with his hind leg, certainly not enough to create a strong jumping canter. If he is pressed, he will accelerate for a few strides, but he still doesn't work any harder than he can get away with.

Tory needs to warm up in showjumping mode and to stop trying to push him forward with her seat and back. She needs to float her seat half an inch off the back of the saddle, which will ensure her weight is hanging down off her stirrup bars, and then her leg can operate with tidy little nudges on every stride. A pushy seat and back indicate to Shamrock that he can tuck his head in prettily and get by with looking a poser. All I can see is a spoofer! A nudge in the ribs to keep him working will have far more effect.

It's very unusual for me to want a horse to have a smack to go forward, and you should *never* smack a horse to send it to a jump, but Tory must give Shamrock a tap behind her leg each time he ignores her when she nudges him to move him. Sidling away half-heartedly is not going to be an option.

Shamrock is very surprised at such a positive move, and shows his resentment immediately by bucking and leaping. However much he prances about, Tory must seize the initiative and keep sending him on. If she checks him back now, she will confuse him and he will associate the smack with a misunderstanding. No matter how much he bucks or protests, the bridging rein keeps her safe because he can't get his head down too far. He must understand that if he doesn't move forward immediately her leg encourages him, he is in big trouble. As long as she is persistent and keeps nagging him, he will eventually realize that the remedy is under his

own control and go forward more willingly. The secret in using this method of improving Shamrock's cooperation is to be totally consistent. Tory must *always* be aware that he might start to backslide and even if he goes nicely for a while, he is eventually going to try to ignore her leg aids again. It is what horses do!

It has a great deal to do with a rider's attitude, and I know how hard it is to be firm with a horse that a rider adores, but he will be a much nicer boy when he is more obedient and hard working, sooner rather than later. The difficult part now for Tory is to realize that a tap might have changed his mind and got him moving more forward, but unless she keeps up with the nudging, the good result that a tap has achieved will be lost very quickly. The tap is to say '*listen*'; it is not a punishment but a warning that he should have a little more respect when he is asked to do something. You must have the right attitude to a stick and use it solely as back up to achieve obedience to your leg, not as a substitute for your leg so that you don't have to work so hard.

The issue is not that Shamrock is reluctant to jump, he doesn't mind jumping at all, and he always manages to bumble over somehow. But he definitely prefers not to work too hard. After discovering a less sympathetic attitude from Tory and a couple of reminders when he starts to be lazy again, he finds the length of the canter poles into the grid easy, striding over each one with his feet in the same position over them all. Tory must *not* tap him as he faces a grid, even though it is very tempting to get a bit more zoom with the stick, but it must be her leg that sends him on and up into a stronger canter. The zoom will give him a bit of speed but it won't make the hind leg work harder, and it is the working aspect that Tory must achieve. It is so easy for Shamrock to canter through the poles when he's working harder. He makes up so much ground with the extra energy, that he is finding the distance easy (Figure 10.4).

a

Figure 10.4 What a difference! A super working canter that promises a lovely jump.

above right and opposite page **Figures 10.5a–c** Even though the jump is good, Shamrock thinks that he has made enough effort and doesn't try very hard to keep it up. The first 'out' pole of the grid should be in the middle of his stride and it clearly isn't.

Tory must now look at the way she is landing after a jump. She isn't timing it well enough to get her leg working quickly enough to nudge him away from the fence (Figures 10.5a–c and 10.6).

Shamrock isn't a spooky horse and has been very laid back about jumping different obstacles or colours. He does not seem to mind what's in front of him, he treats everything the same, and so far his mistakes on a course have been caused purely by him not working hard enough. Often he has been so lazy jumping into a one-stride double that he puts two strides in, and is very comfortable with three strides when he should have done two. It is hard work to jump out cleanly if he is so close to a jump and very uncomfortable for Tory. As for his related distances, he simply hasn't worked hard enough to do the conventional number of strides between fences, which will make his course jumping

a pleasure for Tory. He has been getting away with his extra strides because the jumps are small, but when the jumps are bigger, he will find it more difficult to sandwich in an extra stride and still jump cleanly.

Now Tory has found the right method to make him work better, she must establish his way of going, of working more strongly, while the jumps are relatively small, so that any mistakes can be sorted out before he is asked to compete at a slightly more difficult level. Not only is it uncomfortable for him to creep through his distances, it makes it so much harder for him to get going again after a bunny-hop jump. All the rhythm is lost in an instant, and Tory has to work even harder to move him forward again.

The grid work she is doing is designed to make him work, and to let her know if she is producing enough impulsion. Until he is coping easily with the distances, especially with the canter poles away from the jump, he is not ready to do well round a course of fences. She must not accept that he will get round somehow, and must really nag him to do better. It takes a bit of effort, but until he is moving freely and strongly in his canter, she must not leave the grid to try something else. When he has *worked*

b   c

Figure 10.6 Shamrock is performing a really nice working stride at this 'out' pole because Tory has booted him more quickly after landing from the jump.

properly through the grid, she can have every confidence that he will do better round his practice course. The grid will let her know immediately if she is producing him well enough or not. As long as she keeps up her strong leg and unsympathetic attitude, he should be just as powerful round the track, finding the jumping easy.

Tory must not get him going well and then relax, he will only move and jump better when she keeps his revs up. As soon as she is pleased with how he is going, she may subconsciously ease up a little, which will result in all her good work for achieving impulsion going in an instant. Shamrock will not volunteer to work harder. Eventually he may realize

d

c

h

g

that if he accedes to Tory's nagging he finds the job easier, but she must not bank on him having that sort of logic. He is working harder because she is giving him no choice, and I think that's as far as his understanding goes. Yes, he is finding the jumping easier, but he finds it nearly as easy to pop short strides in and not try so hard. All this bustling and unpleasantness rather washes over him as he doesn't know or understand that one day he is going to jump bigger fences and will be unable to hike his legs up out of the way if he is not going better.

Although Shamrock starts the course well

enough, he manages to sandwich three strides into a two-stride double at number 5. Tory might have been a little slow to push him on landing over the first jump but Shamrock's old work-shy habits surfaced immediately, in spite of working well on the grid. Tory has to take the memory of that grid work with her to his courses and try to reproduce that strong feeling of energy on every stride, not just when she is facing a jump. If she lets him relax and not work hard for a couple of strides, he will look on it as a weakness and try to revert to his lazy ways again. It is going to take a bit of sorting out, but at

b

a

f

e

Figures 10.7a–h Even when he jumps in well and lands in the right spot, he simply won't volunteer to work hard over the first pole and drops short. This makes him reach all the way through and he has to either put a short stride in or a big effort at the second jump. He chooses to be bold and stand off, but it's a long flat jump.

least Tory knows it is not his jumping ability that is at fault, just his attitude to work. He would still like the easier lazy life if he could get it, but he will discover that this is not going to happen.

To convince Tory that he really should be doing

the two strides easily, I put two canter poles down between the jumps (Figure 10.7a–h). Before Tory tries again, she walks Shamrock several times over the poles in the middle so he knows they are there and doesn't jump into the double and back off in surprise.

At least he put in a bit of effort and did the distance on two strides instead of three, but it is still not with the power that Tory needs to produce. Tory works away at this double just as hard as she did with the grid, trying to time her landing and be balanced quickly enough to nudge him up into a strong canter and cover the ground. The canter poles are an invaluable guide for her, letting her know immediately if she has done enough, or not!

It is very satisfying to be able to improve the jumping of the lazy horse, purely with a change of attitude and just a little extra encouragement to work harder, rather than needing to improve the actual technique of the jump. As Shamrock works across the ground in a stronger canter the actual jumps *must* be much easier for him, but he won't understand this or work it out for himself. It will certainly become much easier for Tory as long as she remains not only mentally positive but physically effective with her consistent leg (Figure 10.8).

The only thing she needs to be careful about now is to contain and keep the livelier canter working up, not long. Although he does his flat work nicely in a snaffle, she must be aware that as he goes forward more from her leg when jumping, she must be able to contain all that extra energy so

that it's productive. Once or twice round the course, he has just tugged her very slightly too far forward over his shoulder (Figure 10.9), and if necessary she might need to switch to a three-ring bit (see page 13) so that all the energy can be harnessed instead of running out fast and flat through her fingers.

When the horse is jumping so much better without using any really complicated methods, I don't like to nit-pick and always be looking for trouble, but I can't help it. If I am on red alert for a potential difficulty, then it will probably be avoidable, and just mentioning my concern to Tory will warn her about the hazards of Shamrock going too fast from her leg. She might not realize at first if he is pulling too much for her to contain his power easily, but if she is on the lookout for any new disobedience, she will be able to nip it in the bud. Although it must be marvellous to feel him moving and working better, going faster must not be any more of an option than being work-shy was. (Figure 10.10.)

Figure 10.8 Finally Shamrock works hard enough over both canter poles to arrive at the perfect take-off point with his hind leg about to come down right in the middle of the distance for a strong and accurate effort.

Figure 10.9 This is a nice jump over the tray, but did she voluntarily go a little too forward herself or was she tugged by this much improved horse?

Figure 10.10 Shamrock showing no hint of laziness at a show.

11 Canter poles and the keen novice

Ceilidh and Nicky

Ceilidh is going to work over exactly the same grid as Shamrock (see Diagram 9, Chapter 10) but with a very different attitude. Unlike Shamrock, this horse is very enthusiastic about jumping; she absolutely loves it but is hampered by having a naturally short stride. It certainly isn't impossible for her to cope with the 3.65 m (12 ft) distance but unless Nicky works at it in the right manner and with the right attitude, she will find it hard and confusing.

All the work through this grid is going to be with one purpose, to make use of all Ceilidh's enthusiasm and move her along to lengthen her stride instead of staying up and down and short in her canter (Figures 11.1a–k).

To keep pressing Ceilidh as we did Shamrock (see Chapter 10) is counter productive, all she will do is either go faster or bounce higher and even shorter, and so changing the distance between the canter poles is the method that will produce the best results: *go short to get long* (Figures 11.2 a–l).

Figures 11.1a–k In spite of being very extravagant in over the first pole, Ceilidh lands short and gets shorter and shorter all the way through the grid. Nicky uses plenty of leg to encourage her more forwards but she finds it very difficult. Although she does her best to fiddle the distance, she ends up putting in an extra stride in front of the jump, and then struggles over the 'out' poles.

c

f

i

a

b

d

e

g

h

j

k

Figures 11.2a–l When the poles are moved in to the
3.35 m (11 ft) distance Ceilidh finds it so easy to stay
in the right place in the right rhythm.

c

d

g

h

k

l

Because of the extra impulsion the strength of Ceilidh's rhythm is giving her, meeting the poles correctly is easy, and she actually starts to make up a little more ground towards the end of the grid. Because she isn't stretching, accelerating or fiddling to cope with the poles it gives Nicky a chance to practise timing her nudges to be effective with her rhythm. It is not easy to use your leg consistently when the horse is erratic over the poles, even if she is keen. You won't improve the length of Ceilidh's bouncy and short stride by trying to encourage her to go longer initially. If the distance is shortened to suit her, she will find it easy and stop feel-

ing she has to be so extravagant to try to make up the ground.

The wings have been left in place to show just how much the poles have been moved to suit her, and how even her natural stride can be when she doesn't feel she has to stretch.

This shorter but consistent canter has made Nicky realize just how quickly she needs to nudge to produce the impulsion required to improve the length of stride. When they are both in harmony over the shorter distance, all the poles are very gradually moved back to their original position, by as little as 5–7.6 cm (2–3 in) at a time. It is vital for

a

b

e

f

Nicky to keep up the solid and consistent impulsion, to give the same feeling from her leg every time through the slightly lengthened grid that Ceilidh was receiving over the 3.35 m (11 ft) distance. She can do 3.65 m (12 ft) easily if she allows herself to respond to the consistent nudging from her rider (Figures 11.3a–h).

It's sometimes surprising how simple it is to make a difference to the length of a horse's stride. Ceilidh helps the improvement because she is keen, and very willing to get on with it. Ceilidh and Nicky have worked very hard with this grid and are rewarded with a much better canter and length of stride on the practice course (Figures 11.4a–f). Nicky must try hard to keep that canter consistent by timing her nudges effectively when there are no ground poles to help her judge if she is doing enough. She has to encourage Ceilidh to maintain that slightly lengthened stride until it becomes more of a habit.

Before doing the earlier grid work, Ceilidh would have certainly sandwiched three strides in the middle of the double and been too close to the second jump.

Figures11.3a–h Such a vast improvement from the first 3.65 m (12 ft) grid. Ceilidh is now finding it all very simple as she learns to go forward from Nicky's leg instead of higher and higher.

c

d

g

h

c

b

f

e

You can't change a horse's physique, but you can help improve his stride to become more effective or conventional. Ceilidh has found this course far easier to cope with as her stride has improved in power and length. The energy was already there, but Nicky needed to get the right feel and timing to harness it to be more productive. It is a grid she should practise every time she schools as Ceilidh would find it very easy to just slide back into that shorter, bouncy, natural stride. As the improvement in her jumping is so marked just by developing a better canter, Nicky must keep it up.

So what do you do if your horse has struggled and you have needed to reduce the distance to make him comfortable as we did with Ceilidh? If you've tried Ceilidh's grid and it doesn't help your horse enough when you move the poles out again and if there's no prospect of him lengthening, however much impulsion you give him, then you will have to settle for him popping in two short strides instead of one conventional one in a double measured at 7.3–7.6 m (24–25 ft). You must be prepared to hold him up and accept two three-quarter strides, much as Charlotte does with Jack on page 154. Set the canter poles at a distance at 2.1 m (7 ft) and 5.2 m (17 ft) from the first fence and use them to help you recognize how much support you need to use to hold him well enough off the second fence to jump it easily. But, unless your horse naturally has a tiny stride, you are probably going to be restricted in the size of courses you can jump successfully, purely because you will struggle on your one-stride distances. Obviously there are exceptions, and the more work you do to produce the very short up-tempo stride, the more success you will have in the ring. The canter poles will help.

a

d

Figures 11.4a–f A nice jump in to this two-stride double (number 5 on the practice course), two strong strides through the middle and a perfect take-off point for the out.

12 Canter poles and 'little and large'

Despite their difference in size, Ben and Stewie are competing in the same classes, over the same courses (Figure 12.1). Just like the ponies, at a show both Ben and Stewie are going to be expected to work with the same length of stride through their related distances around the course. It will be the same for both of them. So they both need some help on the grid to produce a conventional stride. Stewie will have to shorten his natural stride of 3.9 m (13 ft) plus, and Ben must work just a bit harder to improve his natural 3.35 m (11 ft) stride.

Ben and Nicky

Ben needs to be encouraged to lengthen only slightly to make his doubles and combinations easier, without having to stretch or pop in an extra stride. He can manage satisfactorily at around 0.8–0.9 m (2 ft 9 in–3 ft) size fences by just popping a little short stride in and making the height out, but he is just a bit too big to be as naturally clever and nimble as the ponies in putting strides in and staying accurate when the jumps are a little bigger. He needs some careful work on the grid with canter poles to help. Now Nicky is more competitive and finds how easily Ben can jump single bigger fences, the only thing that is holding them back is the shortness of his stride in combinations. So far, we have tried to school Ben over a conventional-stride grid with the seven crosses. The crosses have encouraged him to jump, keep going and use himself, and although he found it hard work at first, things improved. When the crosses were reduced to canter poles he didn't need to jump them, so he didn't make up the ground and reverted to cantering on his comfort stride, gradually getting further and further behind as he went down the poles (Figure 12.2).

You couldn't call Ben lazy, just reluctant to improve the length of the stride he is comfortable with to try working a bit harder. The 3.35 m (11 ft) stride is perfectly workmanlike, not idle, but it just isn't good enough for the courses he is going to jump.

Nicky must get the hang of producing a bit more power, which has a lot to do with improving the timing and application of her leg. He needs a nudge at the beginning of his stride, not at the end when it's too late to be as effective.

As you saw with Ceilidh on page 130, the more Nicky C. practised, it encouraged the mare to discover that going forward on the keen stride made the jumping easier than going up and down. Although Ben is pretty co-operative, his enthusiasm for jumping doesn't extend to being bouncy and forward, and it is this sort of canter that the poles will help Nicky K. generate.

If you can manage a single bounce at 3.65 m (12 ft), and most small horses, including Ben, can, with positive and consistent riding and timing you should be able to generate enough power, not speed,

above **Figure 12.1** 'Little and Large: Ben is 15.3 hh, Stewie is 18hh.

Figure 12.2 This is not good enough. Nicky has to ask more strongly, and sooner than this, to make Ben's stride lengthen.

to cope with the conventional one-stride distance. Ben can do this well enough when pressed in the right manner, he isn't a novice but he has just got a bit set in his comfort zone; he really can't be bothered to try a bit harder when he can cope well enough with his little shuffle. Because he is able to do better, Nicky must adapt her technique to insist that he takes the slightly bigger fences in doubles more seriously and works a bit harder in the middle. The jumping then will be much easier for him. As the jump into a double or combination increases in size, Ben jumps bigger and makes up a little more ground in the air and lands a bit deeper into the distance. Of course then it is going to be even more difficult for him to pop in a short stride and still have enough room to be able to jump out well.

Do not just ask for the one stride! If you do, you will go forward with your body and hands and any extra impulsion you've generated from your leg will be lost immediately.

Do not urge him on to get the right effort in the middle. *Do not* try to *make* him take off on one stride. The secret to success is *not* trying to make

him do what you want, but producing so much impulsion so much sooner that it is almost impossible for him to do otherwise. Hold your contact strongly for the two strides! You may be very pleasantly surprised and make the distance comfortably in one stride after all.

Nicky must stay supportive and plan to hold Ben up to be steady but active to do the two small strides he prefers; his confidence will usually grow when he finds he isn't being stretched. Her nudge on landing must be well timed. As long as she supports him with a consistent contact and doesn't get too far forward over his shoulder to try to encourage him to lengthen, his hind leg will be powerful enough to encourage him further forward on the distance. He will find that with a bit more spring, the one stride is achievable. He can't find it easy to get so very close to the second element now he is being asked to jump a bit bigger and he is careful enough not to want to hit poles. He just needs to grasp how much his jumping will improve if he listens to Nicky and stops ignoring the extra leg at the beginning of his stride. If she holds and gathers

a

b

him up enough for two strides it will make it easier for Ben to be more active and get it right in one.

You work with what you have, but the more grid work you do with canter poles to encourage you to ride the stride better, the more chance you have of producing a stronger and more effective canter. Your horse will soon get used to the poles and not make any extra effort to extend over them, but they will be a very valuable indication to you as to whether your timing to nudge is good enough to get the right result.

Nicky hasn't been quite quick enough to nudge Ben at the beginning of his stride, her nudge has tended to come at the end, at the take-off point if you like, and so the stride hasn't been encouraged early enough to be stronger. The canter poles have made this crystal clear and helped Nicky produce a major improvement. (Figures 12.3a–d and 12.4)

below **Figures 12.3a–d** A little more leg, a bit more support and Ben works harder making these canter poles very easy for his stride. It is that strong canter that Nicky will need to produce consistently round a course.

above **Figure 12.4** In the one-stride combination on the practice course, Nicky has just got the balance of leg to hand spot on, resulting in a strong and active one stride to take-off point.

c

d

Stewie and Mary

Stewie has the opposite problem. At 18 hh his natural stride is 3.9 m (13 ft) plus and if allowed to canter normally he makes up too much ground and finds the normal 3.65 m (12 ft) distance too short and so you need to start with the poles at a distance of 3.9 m (13 ft). As you gradually reduce the distances, only 7.6–10 cm (3–4 in) at a time, make sure you have your leg on (Figure 12.5). If you hold the contact too much to shorten the stride without your leg, all you will do is slow him down, not produce the slightly airy bounce to the canter that you should be working for.

The sheer repetition of doing the poles should settle him down and make the stride more conventional, Just persist until you find he canters through and it feels more normal and smooth (Figure 12.6).

opposite page
Figures 12.7a–d Stewie is jumping really nicely in this figure-of-eight grid and Mary is quick to land and pick up the canter and keep it for a successful passage across the diagonal to meet the next jump spot on.

above **Figure 12.5** Stewie is so keen and big. Mary is working hard to keep his canter short (for him) and up.

Figure 12.6 Got it! The pole is right in the middle of Stewie's stride.

Mary needs to drill and drill until the canter is consistently held at the 3.65 m (12 ft) distance and Stewie accepts this as normal. (Figures 12.7a–d.)

It is easier to support a horse to take a shorter stride than push one to take a slightly longer stride but, for both horses, it is the consistency and sharpness of the aids that will do the job. Nicky must push and hold on every stride, and so must Mary; but Nicky must push more and Mary must steady more. They must both always ride from the leg to the hand, and the only difference between their methods in producing the right sort of canter is the varying degree of strength of the leg to hand, how much leg to how much hold. Once that is practised and established they will both jump all the better.

a

b

c

d

13 Ponies

Building double or treble combinations for ponies must be one of the most demanding parts of the course builder's job. There is such a disparity in the length of stride and size and shape of pony.

The British Show Jumping Association's course builders' guide recommends a one-stride distance anywhere between 6.7 m and 7.45 m (22 ft and 24 ft 6 in) for 14.2 hh ponies, which can bring the length of stride just into the same range advised for horses. The two-stride distance is suggested at between 9.75 m and 10.5 m (32 ft and 34 ft 6 in), again just stretching to the same size as a shorter distance for horses. With the smaller heights, the 13.2 hh ponies have 0.45 m (1 ft 6 in) deducted for one stride, 0.6 m (2 ft) deducted for two strides; 12.2 hh ponies have 0.9 m (3 ft) deducted for one stride and 1.2 m (4 ft) for the two strides.

Pony grid-work distances

All the distances prescribed should be used as a guide for setting up your grids and related distances.

All the ponies featured in this chapter have different characteristics. Widget (14.1 hh) and Snoopy (14.2 hh) make up a lot of ground and find the longer limits of the grids easy, as do many other ponies. Jack is 13.2 hh but finds them long and has to adapt his manner of tackling them. Abbie (12 hh) has discovered that she can pop short or long distances easily as long as her rhythm is good. Mitzi (13 hh) is quick and sharp enough to adapt her striding quickly to deal with the fences no matter how she arrives at the take-off point, short or long.

If your pony is struggling to reach the suggested grid distances easily, *do not* try to go harder or faster; reduce the distances until you find his comfort zone and work over that particular distance until the sheer repetition of the work makes it easy for him. Only then should you gradually pull the distances out again, in very small increments, to encourage your pony to work more strongly and to make up more impulsion on his stride, not to reach the poles by faster and flatter.

Smaller ponies can be as clever as cats going round a course, popping strides in to suit the jump, or standing off the fence like little steeplechasers. It is hard to build for the smaller ponies specifically at ordinary shows and so mostly they have to cope with the same distances as the bigger ponies, and they will manage this far more efficiently if they have done their grid work. The grids will make them neater and nimbler so that, when the distances don't suit them, they will have the impulsion and expertise to cope easily, wherever they jump from.

The ideal recommended distances are fine if you are jumping in stipulated-size classes, but if your pony is going to jump in either BSJA ordinary classes such as British Novice or Trailblazer classes for 14.2 hh and under, the ponies will have the same distance to contend with, whatever size or shape they may be.

14.2 hh ponies

Bounce or normal-length stride = 3.35–3.65 m (11–12 ft/3½–4 yd)

One-stride related distance   = 6.70–7.45 m (22–24 ft 6 in/7½–8 yd)

Two-stride related distance   = 9.75–10.5 m (32–34 ft 6 in/10½–11½ yd)

Three-stride related distance   = 12.2–13.7 m (40–45 ft/13½–15 yd)

Four-stride related distance   = 16.7–18.3 m (55–60 ft/18½–20 yd)

Five-stride related distance   = 19.8–21.3 m (65–70 ft/22–23½ yd)

13.2 hh ponies

Bounce or normal-length stride = 3–3.35 m (10–11 ft/3½–4 yd)

One-stride related distance   = 6.25–7 m (20 ft 6 in–23 ft/7–8 yd)

Two-stride related distance   = 9.15–9.9 m (30–32 ft 6 in/10–11 yd)

Three-stride related distance   = 11.1–12.8 m (37–42 ft/12½–14 yd)

Four-stride related distance   = 15.2–16.7 m (50–55 ft/17–18½ yd)

Five-stride related distance   = 18.3–19.8 m (60–65 ft/20–22 yd)

12.2 hh ponies

Bounce or normal-length stride = 2.4–2.7 m (8–9 ft/2½–3 yd)

One-stride related distance   = 5.8–6.55 m (19–21 ft 6 in/6½–7 yd)

Two-stride related distance   = 8.5–9.3 m (28–30 ft 6 in/9½–10 yd)

Three-stride related distance   = 9.7–11.3 m (32–37 ft/11–12½ yd)

Four-stride related distance   = 13.7–15.2 m (45–50 ft/15–17 yd)

Five-stride related distance   = 16.7–18.3 m (55–60 ft/18½–20 yd)

Unaffiliated shows usually have horse strides on 7.3 m (24 ft/8 yd) for one stride and ponies on 6.4 m (21 ft/7 yd). It's a bit of a lottery, and you have two options if the distances don't suit your pony: either do not jump in the classes at all, or you work harder with your grid work to make sure you can cope.

You need to decide a campaign plan and stick to it. The grids will help you develop the necessary method of dealing with your doubles and combinations, whatever sort of pony you are riding, but you will need to remember the method and how to ride when you get to a show.

Build a double at the middle distance suggested for one stride, around 7 m (23 ft), ride through it boldly, and see what happens. Does your pony cope easily on one stride? Does he manage one stride but with a bit of a stretch? Does he have to put in a very short stride to manage, or are two strides absolutely fine? However he copes with the distance you will know what you need to be practising to help your particular pony jump clear.

Snoopy and Holly

Snoopy has a longish stride and you are very fortunate if your pony has a similar stride and can cope with the distance easily. Your method of riding the distance will simply involve jumping in as normal – leg to supporting contact, chin up – and jump out (Figures 13.1 and 13.2). If your pony leaps in boldly, you must hold the contact a touch more in the middle, if you go in off a short stride your leg should still generate enough impulsion to make up the ground easily.

below **Figure 13.1** Snoopy has a long stride and is a keen pony, and jumps easily out over the second part of the double after arriving at the perfect take-off point. It is very straightforward for Holly to stay in balance as all she has had to do in the middle of the distance is to ride as nicely as normal with no extra checking or pushing.

opposite **Figure 13.2** On the practice course, Snoopy finds the distance very much to his liking. He jumps out well.

Holly's grid-work practice for doubles and combinations is very conventional, just repetition to make sure she keeps up the consistency of riding Snoopy forward and up on his non-jumping strides. Basically, they need to keep their eye in and not allow any lazy habits to develop because he does it so nicely. He will only keep doing so well if Holly keeps him up to the mark. (Figures 13.3 and 13.4.)

left **Figure 13.3** At a show, Holly and Snoopy are spot on with their 'out' jump, the distance for him is perfect, so there is no need for overpushing or pulling.

Figure 13.4 Holly and Snoopy don't waste an inch as they take a well-judged flyer over their jump-off planks.

Widget and Elinor

Widget is very keen and bouncy, but he doesn't have such a long stride; he makes up the distance easily by leaping in and doing a bouncy forward stride (Figures 13.5 and 13.6).

Elinor must work hard on the grid to contain his enthusiastic stride and be prepared to steady him in the middle so that Widget's canter stays up and rounded, not fast and flat. She can't afford to let him dictate the speed or he will go too long and too flat. Her timing on landing must be as precise as possible so she can gather him up and produce an 'up' stride in the middle, not a long, flat and fast one. If her timing to steady him is right, everything else falls into place (Figures 13.7a and b).

above **Figure 13.5** Widget has made up so much ground in the middle of the double as he does an elevated canter stride that he reaches the second jump easily at just about the same point as Snoopy, in spite of not having such a long smooth stride.

Figure 13.6 During practice, Widget bounds across the distance to fly out over the third part of the combination. Elinor must be very careful not to let him tug her too far forward.

Figures 13.7 a and **b** At this show Widget gets a lovely shot into the double; he bounded across the distance to the 'out', but found it a little short, Elinor has held him nicely, however, and so he makes a very good job of it.

Mitzi and Elinor

Elinor's other pony, Mitzi, is very whizzy and has a short stride. Elinor never knows how Mitzi is going to stride through a distance until she gets there. If all is well and Mitzi has jumped in big, she will extend in the middle and stand off the second part (Figure 13.8). If she just pops in off a short stride Elinor must be ready for two very sharp strides in the middle (Figure 13.9). Mitzi is well practised in pulling this off, but if Elinor isn't in balance at the beginning of the distance it is sometimes not very comfortable.

Their practice on the grid must be for Elinor to be not too far forward and to try to land in a chin-up position. If Mitzi manages to tug Elinor over her shoulder, she won't be able to produce the long stride and she will be very close to the second part for two short strides. If Elinor can be balanced in time and not over Mitzi's shoulder when she lands, Mitzi will still jump out well, whether she takes one stride or two. (Figure 13.10)

Figure 13.8 Elinor has kept her chin up to stop Mitzi tugging her forward, stayed well back as Mitzi has lengthened across the distance and is ready to support the mare as she prepares to take off from a long way back at the second part.

Figure 13.9 On the practice course Mitzi has sandwiched two strides into the normal one-stride distance between the jumps but Elinor was ready for either option and is still enough in balance to hold her off the last element for an accurate jump.

below **Figure 13.10** Riding over the show course, Elinor and Mitzi have taken the second part of the double easily after only one stride through the middle, thanks to Elinor remembering from the grid work that Mitzi must just be ridden and balanced, not over-organized for her choice of striding.

Jack and Charlotte

Jack is an entirely different sort of pony. He is only 13.2 hh but his mode of jumping is completely different from Mitzi's. He is strong and accurate when he jumps, but very, very steady. He won't zoom at his fences and prefers a very measured approach. When he gets there he has an amazingly powerful jump, but there is no chance of him being able to manage the distance in one stride (Figures 13.11 and 13.12). Physically it's just not possible for him. His natural stride length would be around 2.74 m (9 ft) instead of the more usual 3.35 m (11 ft) for a pony of his size. He's not stuffy, he likes to jump, but he won't and can't extend.

Jack has won a lot of competitions, but only since Charlotte settled down and worked hard to produce the stride he has, to make it work for him and to ask him not to lengthen or go faster.

Initially Charlotte tried to make him go faster to stretch in the middle of doubles but he really won't lengthen or zoom, and all that happened was that he lost his jump and his accuracy. He would do one normal-length stride, and then have to bucket in an incredibly short one to be able to get in the air, finding it very hard to stay clean and go clear. It was most uncomfortable for them both to be tackling that distance on one full stride plus one half stride.

Jack's grid work now is almost exclusively designed to encourage a smooth passage through his

above **Figure 13.11** Jack and Charlotte jump out of the double well on the grid, but he had taken two strides in the middle.

right **Figure 13.12** Again, in the practice combination, Jack jumps out beautifully after taking two short strides.

combination obstacles. At the distance set, Charlotte must plan to ride Jack on two equidistant strides, about three quarters of his normal length.

If your pony's stride is similar to Jack's and you are struggling in your doubles, try this. It will help you jump out of your doubles better.

Canter poles are useful to let you know how quickly you must land and collect your pony to steady for the short three-quarter stride. Once your timing is right and you manage to pick him up immediately and support the first short stride, you'll be in a position to actually push and hold for the second stride. If you can be pushing instead of pulling him back to get the stride in, he will be able to make a good job of the jump out.

Diagram 10 shows you how to set up the grid to sandwich two equi-distant strides. At a 7 m (23 ft) distance the poles are set at 2.3 m (7½ ft) and 4.7 m (15½ ft) from the first jump. It isn't ideal, but it is effective. Ideal would be for your pony to have a longer or bouncier stride, effective is for you to accept your pony's limited length of stride and make it work for you. Certainly it's not easy, but if there's anything you can do to capitalize on your pony's jump, at least you can practise and practise until you're proficient and it starts to be second nature. You are only asking him to shorten each stride a foot shorter than his normal length, much better than trying to push him to do the almost impossible and try to reach the distance in one.

below **Figures 13.13a** and **b** Show day. When Jack jumps into the double as nicely as this (a), Charlotte must be very sharp to gather him quickly for his two short strides. Because he has jumped in so boldly he's a bit deep to the second part, but makes every effort as Charlotte makes sure she's not too forward (b). There is no way he could have covered the distance on one stride, even with such a good shot in, so all that intensive grid work to make him jump better has paid off.

Diagram 10 Jack's grid

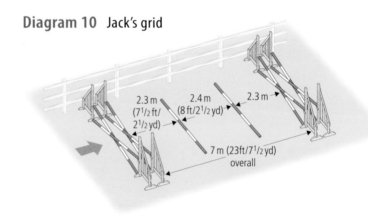

2.3 m (7½ ft/ 2½ yd) 2.4 m (8 ft/2½ yd) 2.3 m

7 m (23ft/7½ yd) overall

a

b

Charlotte has to work with the poles at every training session to remind her how the doubles should be ridden. Jack has few problems with jumping just about everything else and so if Charlotte wants to keep jumping better, she must continue to work hard to overcome his particular difficulty and make the doubles easy for him. The grid is exactly what she needs to remind her how he must be ridden. (Figures 13.3a and b)

It is also the perfect grid work to practise with a 13 hh non-whizzy pony as he will probably be finding the same problem with the distances as Jack.

Abbie and Emily

Emily and Abbie find the 7 m (23 ft) absolutely fine. Abbie is 12 hh and has a very lively and bouncy stride. If she jumps into the double with a big jump, she is perfectly comfortable on two strides (Figure 13.14). If she goes a bit up and down over the jump in and lands short without making up much ground, three strides are not a problem either as long as Emily lands well in balance and keeps pushing and holding. (Figures 13.15 and 13.16a and b)

Figure 13.14 Abbie has cantered two strong strides on the distance between the fences and arrived just right for the second jump.

a

Figure 13.15 Emily has done neither one thing nor another: she hasn't pushed enough for two strides, and hasn't held enough for three. She was a passenger and Abbie has said: 'I can't' not 'I won't'.

above right and right **Figures 13.16a** and **b** Abbie is a little deeper on three strides, but Emily has not tipped forward giving Abbie every chance to come up on a slightly shorter stride to make a good jump out.

b

Emily must work over this grid double and be very quick to recognize how the distance should be ridden. If Abbie again goes a bit up and down at the first jump, Emily must immediately collect her up to be a little steady but moving strongly to allow for three strides. If Abbie goes in boldly, Emily must still gather up but use a little more leg to encourage Abbie to lengthen slightly for two strides.

It is very much a case of thinking on your toes to decide how to ride the striding, but however Abbie lands, Emily must ride a real 'up' canter so she can either hold her contact more for a slightly shorter stride or push on more to make it easy for Abbie to jump out better. *Doing nothing is not an option.*

The hard work is all worth it when everything goes well at a show (Figures 13.17 and 13.18).

Whatever size your pony is and however awkward the double distances may be initially, if you work on the grid and discover and practise the right methods of dealing with the way your pony goes, you will find he will learn to cope easily and jump out well. Be patient and persistent, especially if you don't get the right response immediately. The only way you can help him to jump better is for him to accept that if he listens to how you want him to work on the related distances, he will find it easy. Just make sure you keep telling him the right way to do things.

Figure 13.17 Emily has gathered Abbie up to do two super strides in this double, arriving at the second jump with lots of impulsion.

Figure 13.18 Abbie and Emily in harmony at the show, going just as nicely as when practising at home.

14 Could do better

A keen and enthusiastic horse is a joy to own, as long as he isn't *too* keen or *too* enthusiastic about doing his job properly. Unless you can harness the energy in the most effective way, the horse will become unruly as his natural inclinations to attack the fences may overcome his willingness to listen to his rider; you do not want a 'deaf' horse! And there are varying degrees of deafness: from the horse who occasionally goes a little too fast and carelessly to the absolute hooligan who will refuse to listen to any attempts from you to steady down a bit and concentrate on what he's doing.

Leo and Jo

Q *Is there a way to calm Leo down and make him listen to me?*

A *Yes, of course there is, but it will take a lot of common-sense application to make him understand the ground rules and boundaries you want him to respect. It won't be a quick or easy process for either of you.*

Leo loves jumping, but only on his terms. He is far too keen for his own good and most of the errors he makes are because he is simply going too fast to have time and room to assess the jump (Figures 14.1a and b). Jo finds him difficult to steer and hold him out on his corners beause once he knows where he wants to go he cuts in and leans round the turn, making it very difficult to get a good approach to the next line of fences (Figures 14.2a and b). He works pretty well through a straight grid in the arena, but the inclination to charge off is always there, and the motorbiking he does round the corner is frightening. On a less secure footing, he would simply tip them both over. Her swiftness to take the outside rein has to be improved, but she must be in a position to push him into it to stay upright and balanced, not just try to pull him out.

Canter poles after the grid are essential to help Jo recognize just how quickly she has to land in balance to check him and prevent him getting away from her. The poles will only have a steadying influence if Jo makes it happen as he won't volunteer to behave sensibly. Just holding the contact is not enough if he decides to be onward bound and the canter poles won't make him put the brakes on, but they will help Jo judge Leo's speed and length of stride. She has to be so quick to take the initiative as she lands, otherwise he's gone! He couldn't care less if the poles are in his way or not, he won't let them impede him. But for Jo they are a valuable guide, an indication to let her know if she is doing enough to gather the horse or not.

If the poles immediately out of a grid do make your horse leap over them, there is no chance for you to feel any problems with the actual landing and subsequent strides. If he doesn't settle and

a

Figures 14.1a and **b** a) Leo has charged at this spooky ditch and not spotted it until the last possible second. Because it has taken him so much by surprise he is not ready and leaps out at the side. b) When he comes in at the right speed so he has time to see what the problem is he makes a lovely jump.

b

Figures 14.2a and **b** a) Leo's natural inclination to impose his will makes it a constant battle to keep him up and balanced round a corner. b) When Jo tries hard to square him up and hold him out, he is very resistant.

a

b

ignore them and continues to perform big leaps, try a different method: take them away. Then put a single canter pole on the four- or five-stride distance so that you still have to keep up the momentum and power. Although your horse might leap this single pole because he is surprised to find it there in an unusual position, you will have had a good chance to practise the four or five intervening strides. It is unusual for a horse to continue to exaggerate and elevate his stride (or jump) over a single pole as eventually he will realize there is no need to do so.

However, this is not what Leo needs at the moment. Jo has tried various bits to be able to steady Leo nicely, but he argues with every one. I think whichever bit she uses, he is going to try to thwart her because he wants to, not because her kit is wrong. She has eventually settled on a pelham with roundings as the three-ring bit I recommend for keen or unruly horses makes his mouth sore with its gag action. The pelham can be adjusted via its curb chain, and although he argues with it, he's arguing with the control imposed, not the feel of the bit. She must be able to grab him and pull him up if she has to, otherwise they may both get into a situation that verges on the dangerous because he is so headstrong.

I hesitate to describe Leo as naughty, because he wants to do the job Jo bought him for. He wants to jump, but he must accept that he needs to listen to her, and she must make sure her wishes are conveyed clearly, concisely, and immediately. There is no second chance for her to gather him up once he has shot off, so she needs to nag and persist with the grid work until it drills him into cooperation. There is a different sort of exercise for Leo that will encourage Jo to take charge as soon as he lands and be ready to prevent him motorbiking. He won't approve as it requires cooperation, and so she must get her attitude in gear and be determined not to

allow him to dictate the speed and the steering.

Leo is still asked to do the straight grid and at the short end of the arena, the motorbiking end, I build a little bounce on a curve with diagonal sloping poles with the inside end high and the outside end on the ground (Diagram 11 and Figure 14.3). This extra dimension makes him pay attention and he is a little more receptive to the steering. He has to cooperate if he is successfully going to negotiate the corner well enough to approach the single jump across the arena easily. It is an additional element to the grid work I use very occasionally if a horse is being very difficult. If he is really tricky, it is no trouble to add an extra diagonal pole, also on the bounce distance. The extra bounce on the curve keeps them both a little more level and helps Jo to ride round the turn instead of being towed round (Figures 14.4a–c).

The diagonal pole bounces may be used as a separate exercise to improve your balance and steering if your horse is falling or leaning in on the turn, but you will have more opportunity to use them to greater effect if you set them after a straight grid. The straight grid will send your horse bowling along and so you will need to be extra positive to practise gathering him up at the end of the line before you get to the turn. The turn will come very quickly and if you are too slow you will miss completely and just go wide of the diagonal bounces. If you simply can't get it right, try it a few times without the straight grid first.

If the straight grid isn't there and you can corner 'nicely' and go over the curved bounce properly, what does that tell you? It tells you two very important things: 1. you aren't in control after the straight grid; 2. you must work hard to make sure that you are in control.

Once you can do the end bounces well on their own, introduce a small straight grid and canter poles again, but set the whole thing further away up

Diagram 11   Grid for correcting motorbike turns

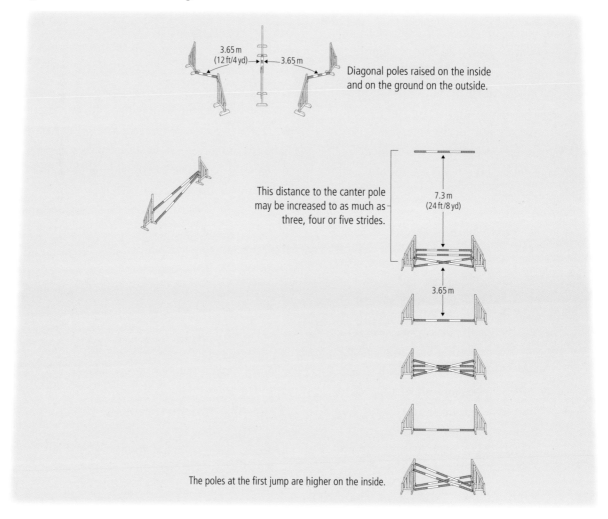

3.65 m
(12 ft/4 yd) ← → 3.65 m

Diagonal poles raised on the inside
and on the ground on the outside.

This distance to the canter pole
may be increased to as much as
three, four or five strides.

7.3 m
(24 ft/8 yd)

3.65 m

The poles at the first jump are higher on the inside.

Figure 14.3 Certainly the bounce across the end of the arena is keeping him much more upright as he goes round the corner. Jo is looking where she means to go, but she must take care not to drop her inside shoulder.

a

b

Figures 14.4a–c It isn't an easy exercise, it's not meant to be, but Leo is working well and is very much better balanced round the short side to the upright on the diagonal. Jo's shoulders are level, the contact is good, and apart from a very minor argument coming out of the bounce, Leo is much more cooperative. He actually looks happy to be doing as he's asked.

c

the arena so that you have two or three extra strides before you turn to the bounces. It just gives you a little longer to establish you are in control before you let the turn come upon you too quickly

Once Leo has worked round this exercise consistently well, Jo takes him on to the practice course to see how he copes with a bit more room. She is determined to reproduce the same sort of feeling and control that she was achieving on the grid, but Leo has other plans. The moment he touches the grass, he wants to be off again (Figures 14.5a and b).

Leo has learned that Jo is not going to allow him to be a thug. It is very hard to be tough on a keen horse, but Jo hasn't been unkind to him, just persistent. If sometimes he has been stopped dead in his tracks, Jo must always remember that the choice to go faster was his, and he must accept the consequences of ignoring her. He won't give in easily, but she will improve both his attitude and his way of going. The sheer repetition of the grid has helped her develop the consistency required to deal with this very able but difficult character. She has made such a good start in establishing some better ground rules for the future, and as long as she doesn't relax her guard things can only get better (Figure 14.6). And get better they do, making going to a show a less nerve-wracking experience (Figure 14.7).

a

b

Figures 14.5a and b a) When Leo bolts off, Jo has to say 'no'. She simply can't let him do as he pleases, and the grid has given her the confidence to insist that he does as she wishes. It is not a pretty picture, but the remedy to this discomfort is entirely up to Leo. He can behave. b) Old habits die hard and he still tries to reassert *his* status quo. Jo must just be a little quicker to tell him not to lean in.

above **Figure 14.6** Very nice. Leo looks happy and cooperative on the practice course, the speed has been acceptable and Leo has had time and room to make a good jump. Chin up, Jo!

Figure 14.7 A good start for Jo and Leo in the show arena.

Bertie and Donna

> **Q** *My eventer always wants to show jump fast. I know this is why she's knocking poles down, but how can I steady her without making her cross?*
>
> **A** *I'm afraid that initially she will be cross when, not if, you try to interfere with her speed but it will make you cross if you keep knocking poles down, especially if you have done a good dressage test.*

Bertie has to accept that she should jump in an up tempo and steady show-jumping canter. It is *not* negotiable, it *will* happen, and Donna is going to ensure that it does.

Bertie needs to do her grid work between competitions in order to be reminded just how show jumpers should behave. She is an eventer, rock solid round her cross-country courses that she loves, but she has sometimes been known to be a little speedy and casual over her show jumps. Usually when I see her the last thing she has done has been the cross-country phase and the next thing she will do is show jumping. It is a see-saw existence for Bertie, she hardly knows what to expect next and so she feels if she jumps everything in her preferred mode, she should be fine. And her preferred mode is the cross-country rhythm and speed.

Donna has to work hard between events to get Bertie to concentrate on the somewhat steadier and more accurate and airy show-jumping phase. After a cross-country run they need to slow down a touch and sharpen up the reflexes to jump cleanly again. The next thing they will jump in competition will be a course of show jumps, and she must be prepared properly if she is to jump clear. She needs reminding that she must go up a little more and along a little less.

The grid to encourage Bertie to just slow down is very straightforward, it works well for her and has the desired effect of making her a bit snappier in front and a little more active behind; or at least it does if it is ridden consistently (Diagram 12).

If your horse is keen but not disobedient when you ask her to steady, you need to be fairly subtle with your aids. You don't want to discourage her enthusiasm; the contact must, therefore, be very consistent, and you must be very careful to keep your leg on as you ask her to slow down. If your leg isn't encouraging the impulsion when you steady, you are in danger of being misunderstood; your horse might misinterpret your signal and put the brakes on completely instead of slowing down.

Bertie is asked to do some seriously hard work on the grid, a grid designed to direct her power up instead of along. If she goes too fast and flat, she will rattle everything and let Donna know just what is lacking from her rider, whether she needs more leg or more contact or both and to what degree of strength the aids should be given to get the best result. As a general rule, more leg will keep the back end springy and more contact will support the front end and make it light and sharper and quicker to snap up. The balance between hand and leg needs to be consistent all the way through this grid and Donna must be very careful not to let Bertie tug her forwards and over her shoulder. If Donna's weight is a fraction too far forwards as Bertie is coming up in front, the mare will find she has more to lift as she comes up off the ground and will not be as free to get up in the air, fold her legs, and jump cleanly.

Step 1 of the grid consists of three canter poles leading to three sharp crosses on the bounce distance and on to three canter poles away. The poles in and out will let Donna know if her canter is consistent and just how much she must steady Bertie's enthusiasm at both ends of the grid.

Once Donna is happy through the bounces and

Diagram 12   Too-fast-to-jump-cleanly grid

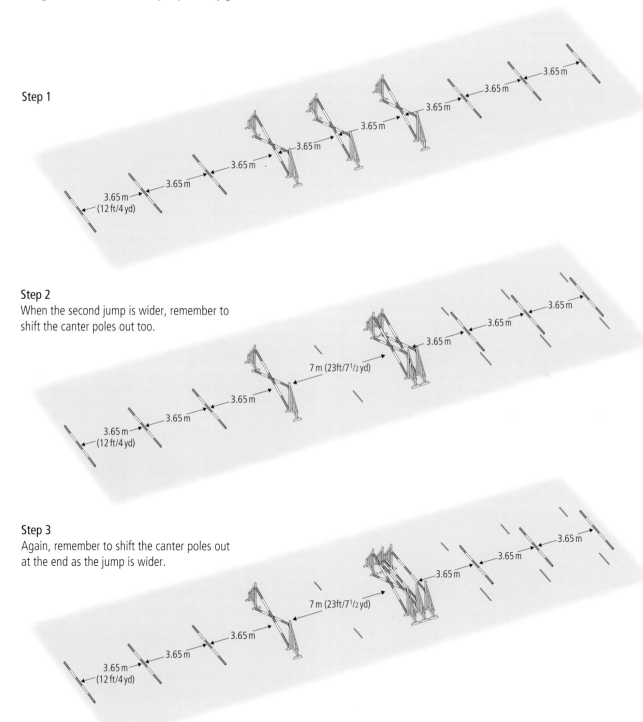

Step 1

3.65 m
(12 ft/4 yd)

3.65 m

3.65 m

3.65 m

3.65 m

3.65 m

3.65 m

Step 2
When the second jump is wider, remember to
shift the canter poles out too.

3.65 m
(12 ft/4 yd)

3.65 m

3.65 m

7 m (23ft/7½ yd)

3.65 m

3.65 m

3.65 m

Step 3
Again, remember to shift the canter poles out
at the end as the jump is wider.

3.65 m
(12 ft/4 yd)

3.65 m

3.65 m

7 m (23ft/7½ yd)

3.65 m

3.65 m

3.65 m

Bertie is making an effort to clear the poles, they move on to Step 2: the grid is made into a double with a single cross in and double cross out, but the canter poles are still used at either end of the grid (Figure 14.8a and b). The distance is made very slightly shorter than normal to encourage Donna to keep hold and Bertie to jump cleanly and steadily.

Step 3 involves making the second jump higher and wider to encourage precision jumping (Figures 14.9a–e).

When Donna practises round the course after the grid work, Bertie is cooperative with the speed and allows Donna to give her time and room to jump cleanly (Figure 14.10).

This grid is excellent for reminding Donna to re-establish the show-jump canter between events. Bertie thoroughly enjoys the work and soon responds to being asked to be a bit steadier and more accurate without arguing.

If you are building this grid, just note that as the jump gets wider, the canter poles on the landing side must move out correspondingly. You don't want to make a nice exit impossibly difficult because you have forgotten to alter the distances.

a   b

Figures 14.8a and b a) The grid is working well. Donna and Bertie make a very good job over this jumble of poles. b) Donna is keeping her upper body up well to stop Bertie towing her fast and flat over the poles out.

a

b

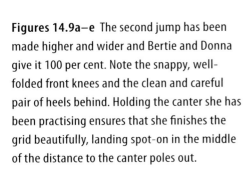

c

d

Figures 14.9a–e The second jump has been made higher and wider and Bertie and Donna give it 100 per cent. Note the snappy, well-folded front knees and the clean and careful pair of heels behind. Holding the canter she has been practising ensures that she finishes the grid beautifully, landing spot-on in the middle of the distance to the canter poles out.

e

Figure 14.10 Bertie is paying attention to Donna's instructions and Donna is able to wait for Bertie's neck to come up to her chest, instead of being tugged over her shoulder prematurely.

Kody and **Mary**

> **Q** *My horse has become very casual with his grid work. How can I make him concentrate again?*
>
> **A** *Easy! Change the look of the grid. It doesn't have to be much more difficult to produce the right sort of effect, it just has to look different.*

Kody is fairly accomplished now with his show jumping and ring craft and doesn't need to practise much over courses at home but he still needs to do his grid work between shows to keep him jumping cleanly, in a focused and obedient manner. Also, if he has had a little hitch at a show, the grid work will set him up nicely again before his next outing.

Kody has been brought up on grid work and normally works well over them. The first two grids in Diagram 13 are fine to start him off but he would

soon become blasé with the familiar work and not try so hard. He is encouraged to take the work more seriously by changing the look of the grid: in the last two grids in Diagram 13 the poles are placed on the diagonal in alternating directions to make them appear far more difficult or unusual and imposing. This grid will make him take more note of what he is doing and sharpen his ideas (and his jumping) up a bit. (Figures 14.11a–c)

This grid is very suitable for fairly experienced horses especially those who become a little know-it-all or too relaxed with the work. Keeping horses supple and obedient between shows is essential but when they are used to the work they can tend to be a little casual about doing the same things all the time. A different appearance to the grid can be very startling. You can see Kody really peeking as he is coming through the grid. It just makes him work hard without you having to build too big a grid. The look of the grid makes him jump better and use himself more and of course it makes him that

Diagram 13 The five-fence-poser grid

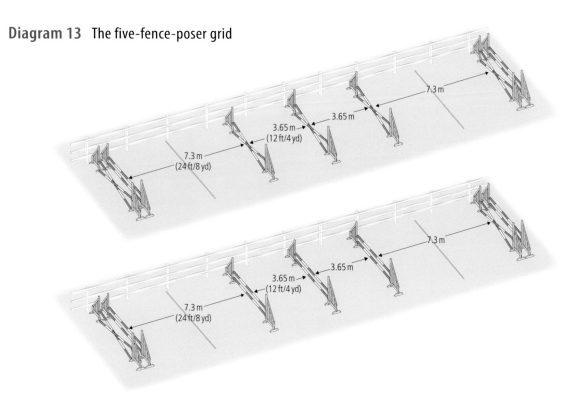

This grid incorporates non-jumping strides plus bounces in the middle. You can remove the middle bounce to make four fences to encourage a good rhythm without rushing. Alternatively you can change the middle, or all three, bounces into low horizontal poles to keep the horse alert.

Another option is to make the middle poles slope alternately.

A very imposing looking grid.

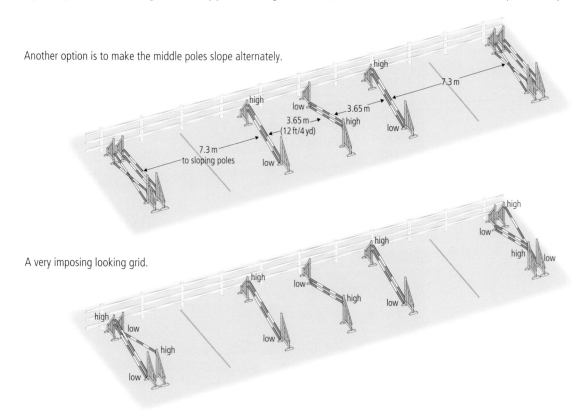

a

b

Figures 14.11a–c a) This diagonally constructed grid is well worth the agony of building it! b) Kody plaits as he tries to keep his feet off this strange looking grid. c) Now the grid is larger it looks quite imposing and encourages Kody to work hard to make a good job of it.

c

little bit spooky which gives Mary a chance to get more leg on and get him going up rather than along. With a conventional grid he tends just to mooch through it, familiarity breeding a little contempt and making him slightly casual, and this grid makes him pay attention. (Figure 14.12.)

If you build this grid at home, the last jump should always have the front poles of the parallel set so that the highest end is to the inside. This should make you straight over the last fence and prevent the clever horse from cutting in too soon.

Figure 14.12 Kody jumping neatly at a show after his serious work on the grid.

Friday and Isobel

Q *In jump-offs, I go fast and often rattle a pole; sometimes out of a double or off a related distance. Quite often it is the last jump; any suggestions?*

A *If you get four faults because you are bowling along, you need to practise your timing. You must be off your horse's front end as he picks up to jump and you also need to have your leg on to obtain spring behind, and more quickly than usual. You need to be sharper with your aids.*

The speed-merchant's grid (Diagram 14) is very good for practising your jump-offs because the rhythm and power required for this exercise will help you assist your horse to get up in the air cleanly when you are going just that little bit faster. But it will only work if you improve the way you ride it. You may want an increase in speed but it doesn't have to cause deterioration in power and accuracy.

If you are up on the clock and in a hurry to approach that last fence, nine times out of ten if you allow a horse to flatten you are going to have the fence down. This grid will help your horse to stay springy, rounded, and careful. You might be going faster but if you practise riding at speed and staying springy you will be able to do enough to get him into the air smoothly. If you sail into a double or a related distance, your speed will bring you too close to the next element. If you aren't quick enough to gather him up, your horse will have it down because you are simply too deep into the fence and too fast for him to snap his forelegs out of the way. Again you want fast and springy, not fast and flat.

When practising with this sort of grid you will improve your ability to instinctively hold off your related fences and last jump even if you are motoring on a bit, or in fact to hold off any jump on your way round a course. If you're in a hurry when you leave the starting gate, you don't just get four faults at the last.

Diagram 14 The speed-merchant's grid
for improving timing

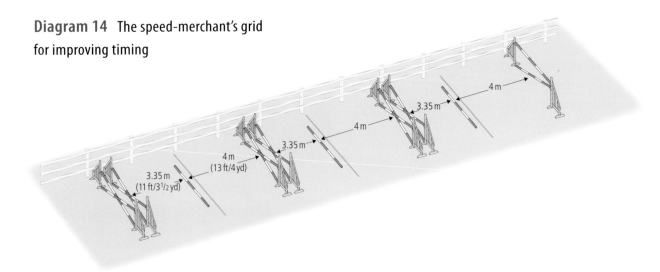

Isobel and Friday are both keen to move on in a jump-off, and are very competitive. Friday loves to go fast and his length of stride increases the faster he goes, making the combination distances very short for him. He has to be ridden and supported on his stride, not necessarily slowed down, but produced 'up' and very active in his canter as soon as he lands.

Isobel needs to use this speed-merchant's grid to develop the right sort of feel for when to quickly gather up and balance Friday to jump cleanly. The distance between the fairly wide double-cross jumps is the conventional 7.3 m (24 ft) and the canter poles set in the grid are 3.35 m (11 ft) from the landing and therefore 4 m (13 ft) from the next jump, all the way down the grid. Double crosses are used to make him stay in the air a bit longer so that Isobel can practise her timing for landing even more accurately. If Isobel anticipates Friday landing and shifts *her* weight to land slightly too soon, even just a split second out, she will shift Friday's balance and he will put a hind toe down too early and hit the poles. Isobel can use this exercise to hone her judgment in the air. If she stays up in her jumping position long enough he will say clean. If she is in a hurry to land to get away quickly from the fences and misjudges her timing, Friday will get four faults.

The distances to the canter poles being a foot shorter on the landing side really makes such a difference, and even when Friday is in jump-off mode it helps Isobel to momentarily steady him very slightly. As Friday lands a touch shorter than normal, Isobel must seize the opportunity to take hold immediately so that she is in a position to ride the stride from her leg. It will help tremendously in a jump-off if she can land and get the same sort of feeling of 'up' at the beginning of his stride, then she will be able to keep the speed up but maintain a nice rounded pushy stride to the next jump. If Isobel is in a situation to push Friday, even when he is already going at jump-off speed he will be much more accurate in his jumping. If she just sends him faster round the course without attempting to keep the power consistent he will not have the spring necessary to clear the jumps. She needs to balance him quickly after every fence so that he doesn't just accelerate away; he must be pushed, and pushed up into a very supporting contact. This is all she would be trying to do at a normal first-round speed, the principles of producing impulsion do not change, but at jump-off speed, everything needs to be done a split second sooner if you are going to avoid knockdowns.

The short-landing pole will help check him very slightly, and it will also act as a guide to help her feel just how much leg and contact is required to be able to push on (Figure 14.13). She must do the same and operate just as quickly when there is no pole to help steady and collect Friday more at the beginning of his stride. The split-second improvement in the timing means Isobel can say 'come here' as she lands and get the right response. Unless Friday is gathered up and then sent forward, in the smallest fraction of a second, he will think it is great fun to be allowed to charge heedlessly round the jumps at his own speed. He doesn't need any encouragement to zoom about, he loves it. If he is too fast or too deep into the fence to snatch all his legs up in time it is not a disaster, for him, just a minor inconvenience. All he knows is that he's being unruly and having fun.

If the poles were in the middle of the distance as normal and Isobel encouraged Friday to increase his speed he would just bowl on and flatten away to the next jump. In order to go faster round the jump-off fences you need to understand the mechanics and timing of the canter. If you are in a position on landing to give a little more support immediately to counteract the bad effects of going faster, i.e.

Figure 14.13 Isobel is going fast and has timed her landing well to use the effect of the shorter distance of 3.35 m (11 ft) to the pole. Then she is able to be push on and ride forward to the next fence, instead of having to check immediately in front of it. It is all in the preparation and timing. If you are going to go faster, you need to practise keeping the horse jumping cleanly, giving him a fraction more time and room before he takes off by riding a more thoughtful and positive landing at the previous jump.

knocking poles off with a flat jump, you will be able to push to the next fence instead of being towed to it, however many strides away it is (Figures 14.14a and b). If you are pushing and supporting to the right degree and you don't lean too far forwards in your enthusiasm to do a better time, you will jump precisely.

Once again the schooling work pays off in the show ring (Figures 14.15a and b).

Q *How can I decide when Friday is OK to jump higher and wider tracks?*

A *Try jumping higher and wider on the grid first.*

You will both feel secure and confident with a familiar exercise and should build the last fence on the grid higher and wider gradually until it is larger than your normal exercise finishing point.

a

Figures 14.14a and b In jump-off practice on the more demanding arena course, Isobel has really sent Friday on across this dogleg related distance from numbers 4 to 5. The conventional number of strides for the sensible route is five working strides but she has cut in to her left, taken a stride out, and still jumped very cleanly at this awkward parallel. Note how she is already looking for the next jump.

b

a

b

Figures 14.15a and b a) Isobel and Friday fly round the jump-off, staying clean, and Isobel looks for her sharp turn. b) The winning round.

If Friday is happy and keen and jumps the bigger grid fence easily, jump it a few times so that you can both get your eye in and the jump doesn't look imposing to you. Then try jumping the same bigger grid fence on its own without using any of the earlier poles that have helped you arrive at the most beneficial take-off point. Try very hard to keep the rhythm and impulsion to the fence, and don't panic if the take-off stride isn't what you hope for. Just stay cool and allow Friday to use his scope and power. You must not ask Friday to jump the bigger fence by trying harder yourself, as you should already be working at maximum power anyway, even over the smaller fences; just make sure you don't put *less* effort in. Friday needs the consistency that you have

established, and if you change things when the jumps get bigger he will change too, and he won't have enough power to make the jump easy for him. If you can't resist trying to help more, use your legs, not your body and hands, to encourage a bit more 'jump'. More leg but no more speed should keep the confidence intact and you should sail over your jump, wherever you have taken off from. You really don't need to impose your idea of the take-off point on him, give him the power and he will get it right. For Friday it will always be right if you ride him

Figure 14.16 There are no problems here as Friday and Isobel happily pop over this bigger fence in complete harmony.

consistently all the way to the bottom of the fence with the same leg to hand. If you try to adjust the power because you think you will be too deep into, or too far off, the fence, all you will succeed in doing is distract him at the point where he needs to be concentrating most on the job in hand.

If all goes well, put your practice course up a little higher and wider than normal but not too high or too wide, just up one hole on the wings and 7.6–10 cm (3–4 in) wider. Do not, however, take the fences as high or as wide as you have been doing with the grid; you want to encourage him to do more gradually, not by using shock tactics. If you have prepared him to jump bigger fences properly, he will be fine as long as you stay the same consistent rider he is used to (Figure 14.16).

B and **Nicky**

Q *When I practise grids at home, B soon stops paying attention. Is there anything I can do to make her concentrate better?*

A *This is a similar problem to that which Mary had with Kody but you don't need to go to the trouble of building such a complicated grid as the one Kody used.*

B is immediately suspicious of any tiny change, and Nicky needs to plan to have someone alter the middle section of the grid each time she goes down it to keep B paying attention at every effort.

B works nicely at first down the fairly demanding

five-fence-poser grid (see page 171). It is hard work for her as the crosses are quite sharp and she soon becomes casual and careless. It is time to alter the cross in the middle to horizontal poles; they don't need to be too high, certainly no higher than the middle of the original cross, but they must be different looking to make B pay attention once more (Figures 14.17a and b).

The effect might not last more than two or three efforts, and so change a different cross to a horizontal pole instead or even in addition to the one that's already there. At that height three horizontal jumps on the bounce distance in the middle are perfectly acceptable, especially if you get your horse jumping better. To keep B working well, Nicky needs a bit of variety, not by making the grid much

Figures 14.17a and **b**
a) B immediately pays more attention as she spots the difference in the fences and you can see how she snaps her front legs up very neatly.
b) B's nippier all the way down and makes a very extravagant leap out over the last jump.

a

b

more difficult – it is already pretty demanding if B works properly – but by altering the appearance of the grid in order to make her prick her ears and take notice of the changes. Altering any or all of the three middle crosses will produce the sort of improvement and extra effort all the way through that B gives over the last jump.

CJ and Shelly

> **Q** CJ's rushing again, how can I get him to listen to me?
>
> **A** Canter poles will certainly help this 'deaf' horse as well.

CJ has been unruly in the past, and after a long lay-off, he looks as if he might be going down that road again. Shelly has started him off with all the right work. After a long break, the basic 7 crosses are virtually guaranteed to refresh his memory and are the perfect exercise to remind the horse how to work hard and be accurate, neat and nimble. The

crosses certainly contain CJ's enthusiasm, but once they are made into a combination, he starts trying to tow Shelly along faster and faster on the non-jumping strides. She is simply not quick enough to steady him at the beginning of the stride to stop him from speeding up, and so a bit of work on her timing is prescribed.

CJ is asked to work over this long grid, a jump in to 5 canter poles on the 3.65 m (12 ft) distance to another jump out again. For good measure, there are also canter poles away from the grid too (Diagram 15).

If he puts one foot wrong, long and/or goes too fast Shelly will know immediately and hopefully be in position to say, 'No, wait for me.' (Figure 14.18)

The canter pole exercise is ideal for Shelly because it gives her the confidence to know she isn't misreading the situation. If he charges on on a related distance and she is unsure about how strongly she should check to stay balanced and in control, the awareness of where the canter poles should be in relationship to his strides tells her all she needs to know. She won't over-check because she can recognize if things are acceptable or not as they happen (Figure 14.19).

Diagram 15   Rushing-on-the-related-distance grid

Use the canter poles to help you recognize how much you need to do to keep the rhythm.

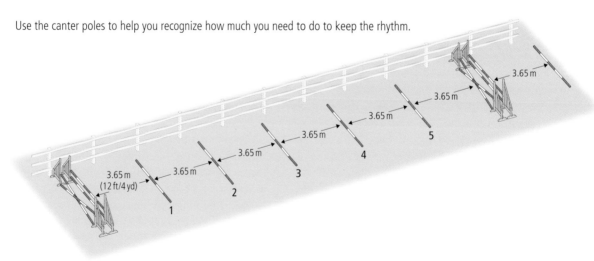

3.65 m
(12 ft/4 yd)   3.65 m   3.65 m   3.65 m   3.65 m   3.65 m   3.65 m

1   2   3   4   5

above **Figure 14.18** CJ has sailed into the grid and Shelly really has her work cut out to steady him in the middle. They might well be at odds with each other but she *must* keep nagging until he gives way and lets her decide the speed.

above right **Figure 14.19** When Shelly gets it right, CJ gets it right!

If your horse starts to rush like CJ after a break, do understand that a lot of the enthusiasm stems from the fact that he's glad to be doing the work again. Don't begrudge him this treat, just be prepared to work through the problem rather than bully him. One by one, remove the canter poles starting with number 3, then 2, then 4 and 5. Leave number 1 pole till last so that you still have a guide when you land to gather your horse up. Be very patient with him. If he starts to quicken and/or lengthen again, replace the pole you have just removed and work until he settles once more. You could need more than one session of this work to get him cooperating again, but it will be well worth it.

Remember that when your horse has been schooled with conventional and repetitive grid work, he will soon get back into the swing of things after only a few grids. If he is very fresh the grids will soon settle him to working over jumps again and it is unlikely you will need to backtrack much.

Q *Because CJ's rusty, and I am too, do I need to go back to the original exercise of working him over poles on the ground to make him more careful again?*

A *Yes, and a very useful exercise it was and still is.*

After a break, CJ just needs to be reminded that kicking poles out is not an option. When he started jumping he was very sprawly and gangly, and even with a lot of patience on the grid, he would not pick his feet up. He just clattered through with no respect for the poles at all. If he met the poles at the easiest point of his stride, he would canter over them, sometimes clearing them, sometimes not. If he had to put himself out to try harder, he didn't; he just ran straight through them. Because he is big and strong, he barely noticed they were in his way; he just pushed them out and carried on unperturbed.

This attitude is only helpful in as much as he never spooks at anything, an obstacle to him is just that, an obstacle to be negotiated, whatever it looks like. Shelly tried using different colours, fillers, all sorts of nice ways to make him respond, but it didn't happen. We needed to try something a bit more basic to make him jump better.

When he was going through (literally) the grid, Shelly would grit her teeth and say nothing, we both hoped he would learn and do better, but all the examples of 'Come again but with more…' simply were not working. If CJ understood that Shelly was getting exasperated, he didn't let it trouble him at all, and he certainly didn't know he was being obtuse and awkward by kicking poles all over the arena.

So, he had to be told. Teaching him not to touch the poles is such a simple thing to do, but it needs *consistency*. You must be on the alert for any backsliding and correct it immediately. I suppose it took half a dozen short sessions with poles at home to produce a reformed character, and it is something you can do easily on your own. It doesn't involve leaving the ground, just making sure your horse knows that you don't like him touching poles and, after a long break, Shelly just needs to remind CJ what the rules are again.

If your horse plays 'tappy-toe' and needs to be corrected, and you riding better isn't solving the problem, try the following.

Put three or four poles on the ground at random, not too close together and not in a straight line, just throw them down and use them where they land. Walk your horse over the poles and if he touches one, even with the tiniest rub, make a real hullabaloo. Shout, growl, hiss, slap your boot (not him) with your stick at the same time, and really let him know you are very, very cross! Think of how you react if he stands on your toe deliberately or swings round to nip you. I am sure you say something a

bit sharp to let him know he's being naughty. So say it now!

He will be amazed you are making such a fuss, and wonder what he's done to deserve it, but he'll soon discover what's precipitating all this unpleasantness, or he will if you keep it up. You *must* make this fuss *every time* he touches a pole, however faintly you hear it. Don't give up on this exercise; think how much aggravation it will save you in the future. If your horse knows he is in for a burst of criticism each time he touches a pole, the remedy is in his own hooves. He can pick them up.

Often this treatment works well on the nice horse, the horse that is going so sweetly but still manages to finish a round with two or three poles down. Because the horse is sweet and willing and because you feel you have ridden as well as possible, you don't like to find fault but if your horse isn't told clearly that you don't like him touching poles, how will he know? It is very easy to blame yourself for any knockdowns as mostly it *will* be your fault, but it will certainly be an asset if he tries hard to pick his feet up even if things aren't quite perfect for him in terms of the impulsion you produce or your balance over the fence.

You *know* that walking over a pole on the ground is not too demanding and so you can rest assured that you are not touching poles because the jump has been a bit big for him, or you have ridden badly. But you must take the exercise very seriously. Once he knows that it is the rattle of a pole, once he makes the connection that this is causing all the drama from the rider, he should start to improve and try harder. But he will only try as hard as his rider. When I've started someone off with this exercise, it works very well to begin with; the rider is focused and responds immediately to a rub of a pole. But once the horse has walked over the poles cleanly four or five times, he will start to relax, put all the nastiness behind him and think you aren't going to keep it up. He will become casual once more, not because he is being naughtier than he was in the beginning, but because his attention span has slipped, and it is easier to be sloppy.

This is where most riders fail with this exercise unless they are reminded to keep up to scratch. If the horse has been working well, they tend to ignore a very slight rub but it is even more important to tell him off once he has started to be more careful and then backslides again. If your signals are mixed, he won't learn, he will always think he might have the option to work casually again unless you make sure he understands otherwise. Get tough and stay tough. You will be surprised at how well the attitude you are producing, the 'try harder' syndrome, will transfer from your ground poles to your grid work and courses. A pole is a pole, whether it is on the ground or in the air. Using the ground poles at walk will help you establish the principle of not touching

them, and you must then be prepared to grumble heartily at the first sign of him rubbing them when you are jumping.

This is why it is so important to use your voice at the same time you flap your stick. Your voice will soon be enough to tell him off (Figure 14.20). It is quicker to growl than slap your boot at the first hint of a rub, and far more acceptable and tidier in the ring.

You should do this exercise for a few minutes every day for several days, or as long as it takes to get the right reaction (Figure 14.21). It is all rather boring and repetitive, but do you want your horse to understand he should jump cleanly or not? Of course you do; however unrewarding this exercise seems to be when you start. He will take his cue from you, and if he understands *clearly* what it is you don't like, he will find it easier to try harder to jump better.

left **Figure 14.20** CJ doesn't like to be told off for touching a pole, but he needs reminding not to do it.

above **Figure 14.21** Not a hint of a rattle through the demanding practice combination: fence number 3.

Legend and Abi

Q *How can I persuade Legend to be steadier with his show jumps?*

A *You have to tell him because it isn't just Legend who likes to go fast!*

Legend is an eventer, and Abi is keen. Their favourite phase is the cross country, and he sometimes spoils his show-jumping round by rushing on between his fences. They both like the cross-country speed but Abi knows she must steady him a little as he zooms away from one jump and gets a bit too

Figures 14.22a and b As Legend works through the grid, the poles on the way through help Abi keep him steady, but as soon as he jumps out he charges off round the corner, too fast and too flat. When Abi tells him to slow down, he argues.

close to the next one to pick up his feet in time on a related distance. Legend will also use a turn to seize the initiative and tries to tow Abi round the corners to take control and accelerate. He is nowhere near as strong willed as Leo, but he is fairly experienced and likes to take charge. He is sure his way is best but Abi must learn to say 'wait' as they land and mean it (Figures 14.22a and b).

Abi has to realize that if she doesn't interfere, Legend is just going to hurdle round his show jumps, and she needs a pointer to let her know just how much she has to do. If she's quicker to land and take charge on landing to stop him cutting in before he gets going, it will certainly make the show jumping better. A pole set not too far from, and at a right angle to, the corner will make sure she holds him out more to be square and steadier off the turn (Diagram 16). It lets her know just how quickly she needs to pick him up after a jump to stay in control of the speed. Of course he doesn't approve, but after a few practice exercises, he starts to be a little more cooperative (Figures 14.23a and b).

a

b

Diagram 16   The riding-the-corners grid

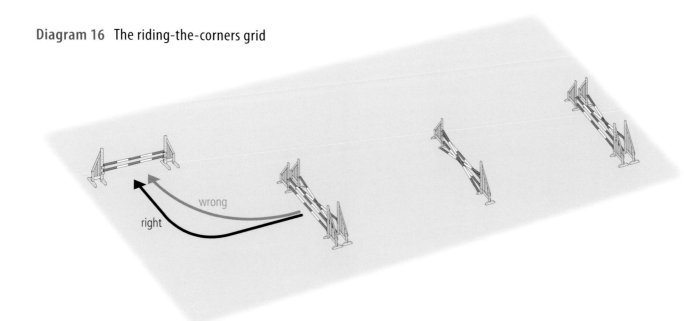

below **Figures 14.23a** and **b** a) Abi has nagged away, told him firmly, and he is gradually starting to give in. b) This is really nice, Abi has control of the speed and steering and hasn't let him cut in.

a

b

When Legend started to work on the practice course in the arena, however, he once again started to try to take charge (Figure 14.24).

Legend gave her no chance to pick him up quickly enough and he shot across the four-stride distance to the triple bar, making it very short. If it had been an upright or a true parallel instead of a 'staircase' jump he would have been in a muddle, purely because of his enthusiasm. Abi managed him well round the rest of the course and she kept him steady enough to jump cleanly, even though he had to snap a little sideways to get it right out of the combination (Figure 14.25). He is so eager to zoom on and round the turn.

Abi must be two steps ahead of Legend and just not allow him to take charge (Figures 14.26a and b). He isn't that argumentative and, of course, Abi's inclination is to enjoy jumping at speed, but if she wants her show jumping rounds to be clean, she must buckle down and practise this sort of work until it becomes second nature to them both.

Figure 14.24 Abi contained Legend well until he really powered over jump number 5, the double.

a

above left **Figure 14.25** Note that Abi is level although Legend is leaning. She is preparing well to hold him out round the next corner.

above right and right
Figures 14.26a and **b** Legend is asked to repeat the hurried four-stride distance between jumps 5 and 6 with the canter poles giving some help to Abi (a). He isn't pleased but the poles have helped Abi realize just how much he was previously taking advantage. When she's in charge, he jumps well. Note how she is looking round the corner to prepare to hold him out and get the steering and speed right.

b

Frankie and Diane

> **Q** *I'm having a job stopping my horse cutting corners. What should I do?*
>
> **A** *Keep a supportive outside rein.*

Frankie cuts corners because he's very pleased with himself and he's sure he knows where he's going next. Once Frankie has seized the initiative, Diane has an argument to deal with as he gets crabby, swishes his tail, and really fights her to get round the corner sooner. It is hard to be balanced and jump the next line of fences well as he is concentrating more on getting his own way than on that which he is going to face next. As in most cases of horsy non-cooperation, prevention is far better than cure. If Diane thinks Frankie is more likely to try this than not, she should be able to overcome his youthful arrogance without too much trouble.

If your horse cuts corners – and do remind yourself that this is something that is triggered by enthusiasm to get to the next fence – try to be a little more watchful and forward thinking as you approach any turn. It only becomes a nuisance when you have to correct him after he has cut in, so try hard not to let it happen in the first place.

Take hold of the outside rein more strongly well before you are anywhere near the turn; if you persist in making sure he doesn't cut in well in advance it won't start to happen. If you wait until you get the tiniest slant and then try to correct it, you have an argument on your hands which could have been avoided. Like so many situations with horses, if you are on guard to foresee and prevent a

Figure 14.27 Sometimes his enthusiasm to turn can work in your favour. Frankie is more than willing when asked to cut in to the right on this jump-off turn but Diane is looking where she means to go, keeps her inside shoulder braced up and maintains a very supportive outside rein.

resistance, it simply won't happen. When you think he's going well, it is then that you relax and forget to be quick enough to stop things going wrong; and they will go wrong. He is a horse, and unless you continually make him work and cooperate, he will try to do his own thing. You must understand that he's not being naughty, he just thinks he knows it all, and he knows where he's going, he wants to get on with the jumping, and he is in a hurry. Of course, he doesn't realize that if he cuts a corner, he is not going to have room to get a good line to his next set of fences. But you do! It is up to you to prevent it happening, and you must work on feeling the outside rein every time. Don't make him go well and then expect him to keep it up voluntarily. He may do what you want but he thinks for himself, and if you allow him the choice he will still cut the corner, no matter how many times you've done it well, simply because he wants to. Don't give him the opportunity to catch you out. If you want a short turn, make sure it's on your terms. (Figure 14.27)

15 Bogey jumps

Q *My horse doesn't like water trays/triple bars/stiles. How can I give him more confidence?*

A *Perhaps your horse doesn't cope with these obstacles so well because you don't like the look of them.*

How can you instil confidence in a rider to approach an obstacle if they think the horse will not like the look of it? If the rider is suspicious of something, the horse will immediately pick up on the fact that this obstacle is something to be wary of.

Very often when I'm training someone new, or if I put a fresh or extra-bright jump out on one of my courses, I see the rider sidling around the jump as they warm up and encouraging the horse to look at it, especially if it is a tray or water jump. They are anxious that the horse might be spooky or nap at something more unusual and so they want them to have a good look first. I can understand this logic, but it is the *rider's logic*, not the horse's viewpoint.

When a horse goes somewhere strange to train, or to jump at a show, all the jumps are new to him. If his rider chooses a jump to make a fuss over and shows it to him, *his* logic will often kick in and he will wonder why? Surely if his rider goes to all that trouble to show him one jump when there are ten others, then maybe that jump really is something to be worried about. He then regards it as suspiciously as his rider. If your horse has a history of refusing or

napping at a water tray, however, then obviously you are right to be careful and ready for trouble, but showing him the disliked obstacle is pre-warning him and letting him know you are worried. It gives him the chance to prepare to be frightened or naughty, whichever technique he uses to be evasive.

If you let him peek and spook at one jump, you should proceed to let him put his head down and look at all the rest; don't concentrate on just the one jump, show him them all. But, better still, show him none! This is by far the most sensible option, and you should train yourself to not show any difference in your determination at the disliked jump when warming up. Have a determined approach to them all and get him into the habit of being obedient. If you change your style of riding at a jump you don't like, it sends an immediate signal to your horse that a change in his behaviour is expected, and usually he will oblige.

Water trays/jumps

The water tray, or wider water jump, is the one that causes the most trouble with refusals and you may worry about getting over them at all, let alone jumping them better.

A lot of misunderstandings and bad behaviour are caused by riders anticipating their horse's dislike of the hazard, but often they are right to be anxious. If the initial water tray practice has been unsuccessful and unpleasant, the horse will often dig his toes in and refuse to cooperate. There are three main reasons for your horse to be silly and difficult, so you must try to get into his head and work out the reason and how to encourage him to be bolder, or better still, indifferent, to any low-lying hazard like water trays.

1. The novice horse might not like it because he is timid and suspicious of everything new.

2. The rider might not like it because of an unfortunate previous history with another horse. This is quite understandable, as bad experiences with horses tend to stand out in the memory, and however hard you try, these thoughts are not easily pushed to one side. This horse will then realize that the rider is anxious about his behaviour, and worried that he might not jump.

3. The horse might have a genuine fear of, or reason for not wanting to tackle, water jumps or trays, because he has had a bad time in the past.

Whatever the cause of his suspicions or dislike, you are the one who is going to have to sort it out, and you must plan your campaign methodically, leaving nothing to chance. The reasoning behind your approach will work whatever the cause of his resistance.

If your horse has not had a bad experience and is just being timid or really silly and won't consider going near the jump, make sure you have someone on the ground to help you, preferably someone the horse knows and likes. Be prepared for a long and patient session and make sure your attitude is positive. If you let yourself become exasperated because you are taking a long time to get a result, all the patience you have shown up to that point will be wasted. The same attitude must apply to curing all three reasons for napping or refusing, and the method will be the same. It won't be a quick fix,

it never is, but if you do it properly, you should succeed long term, not just on the day.

Start off with a small, plain, fairly narrow tray on the ground between wings, and with no poles and no water. It would be very sensible to position the jump so that you will tackle it heading towards the gate or exit.

Exaggerate looking up as you approach it in trot, *not* in canter. The steadier you are, the more chance you have of success. In canter, it is far easier for your hands to move and yield in rhythm with his stride, especially if he is backing off, and he only has to drop his nose to peep at the fence and all the energy generated is lost. Stopping will be easier than going! It will be very difficult not to look down but if you do, your hands will again give slightly and you will lose all the power and energy generated from your strong leg.

In trot you stand much more of a chance to keep him moving forward, and if he does spook violently or try to shoot sideways, it will be easier to stay in the saddle at a slower speed. Don't give him the option to be silly and nip out at the side but, if you are slow to keep him straight and he does run out, *do not* let him continue the way he has chosen. Wherever you are on the arena, turn him back on himself and then retake your track. If you go round in a circle, it will be a victory for him, and he will continue to try the running-out nap every time. If you prevent him from going the way he has chosen, it will be half a victory for you. Remember, if he runs out, it is because he can, because you've allowed it to happen. If you keep him straight he might stop, but stopping has a different remedy. You will be able to deal with that more positively than you can deal with him shooting off into the distance because your steering has not been reliable enough.

If he stops, hold him facing the tray and nudge and kick away until he responds. If your horse is a real baby, this is when you need your helper; you might find that a timid horse will respond to a lead.

Prince and Angela

Angela's horse Prince is a real novice and very spooky. He has always been suspicious of anything new, and although he is now very good at his grid work and doing well in competitions, he will often drop back to trot to give him time to assess the situation. He will usually jump as his whole method of training has been to give him no options. He knows he mustn't turn away as in the past we have dismantled anything he doesn't like and taken it right down to 46 cm (18 in) and nagged him until he has hopped over from a standstill. He has had to go forward. He does, however, really get stuck at the tray. Angela's husband Ian is retired and spends a lot of time with Prince; they are good friends and Prince knows him well and trusts him. Ian is therefore the ideal helper for this exercise. In this situation a trusted friend, especially one who dishes out sweeties, is the perfect assistant and, although a stranger to the horse is not the best person to try to help, a stranger is better than nobody.

Prince watched as Ian approached the tray. Ian let Prince see him stand on it and walk up and down on it to show the horse that there was nothing to be afraid of. It shouldn't be any more worrying than a wooden ramp. Angela must keep Prince facing the tray as Ian walks past the horse and steps on and then over the tray. She keeps kicking and hopes that he gains the confidence from his human friend to walk up to and hop over the tray; trot is clearly not an option because Prince is too suspicious.

If you are in this situation, don't let the helper grab the bridle or reins, you want him there to give reassurance, not to give conflicting signals to the horse. Trying to pull him over must not be an option. Neither do you want the helper trodden on or barged into; make sure you keep the helper to the side and the horse straight. You are showing him very clearly that there are no real dangers, and that must be enough. At the end of the day, he still needs to listen to *you*, however much he is relying on his friend to show him there's nothing to worry about (Figures 15.1a–c).

If you are working this way, make sure your helper nips over the tray and cuts off to the left without looking back to see if it works. Ian has every confidence in Prince not jumping on him, but I'm afraid I am much more cautious. He is putting himself at risk as he is so keen to see if it works.

This method usually works with a young inexperienced horse or pony especially if he is anxious rather than obstinate. He won't want to say no when the instructions are clear and strong, and giving him a lead will offer him the opportunity to change his mind. Your helper might have to walk past him and over the tray several times, but give it a chance to work. Normally he will be relieved that the solution is really quite simple and you must make a fuss of him when he responds, but keep coming round, following the helper several times, until you feel that he is ready to go over the tray on his own. If he does that's good, but if you have asked him a little too early, bring the helper back again. Don't stop too soon after achieving your aim, he is only walking and hopping the tray, so even if you think you have done enough, don't relax until you have encouraged him to jump from both directions. When you approach the tray from the other side, however well he has been cooperating, get the helper to give him a lead. Horses will rarely go as well immediately with a change of direction as they always look on it as a fresh fence or obstacle. This isn't unusual, and you will already have found in your grid work that a change in direction means a

a

b

c

Figures 15.1 a–c a) Prince is watching Ian as Angela nudges him to follow. Ian shouldn't have looked back as turning to face Prince might have halted his momentum. Prince must not get left behind, he must follow Ian's continuously moving lead, which will also ensure Ian does not get jumped on! It is always an unpredictable situation, nobody is sure how quickly or extravagantly Prince will react. b) Prince has followed Ian like a lamb and been very brave but I'm horrified to see Ian still in the way and actually making Prince detour round him; this is definitely not advisable. c) This is really risky, Ian must get out of the way before he turns back to see what's happening.

slight alteration to his way of going, however well he has done so far. He is certainly not going to like the change of direction at a hazard he was not very pleased with in the first place. Just nag away, give him no choice, and you should find he will give in and behave fairly quickly once he recognizes that you won't give up and that there is very little to worry about, whichever way he looks at it.

Once he is going freely, go back to your original direction and add a pole to the jump, low enough for your helper to be able to step over it still (Figures 15.2a and b). You want the horse to look on the tray as a jump, nothing more or less.

It might be hard work and if you have no help you might be tempted to pick up your stick and flap at him in encouragement to make him go forwards,

but *do not* do it; don't use a smack to make him go forward. You must kick him, big thumping gymkhana kicks if necessary, to go forward from your leg. This is no time to be subtle with your legs. As long as he is stationary, nag and kick to move him on.

If he takes one step back he will be napping, which is a very different situation. If he takes even the tiniest step backwards, take your hand off the rein and smack him on the bottom. Use a stick with a split flapper so that it makes a noise rather than hurts. You don't want to hurt him, it won't work and may make him more resistant, but you have to show disapproval if he goes backwards, you cannot sit there and accept it without letting him know he is being naughty. If he keeps moving in reverse, keep up the smacking, not hard but persistent.

a

Figures 15.2a and **b** As soon as Prince sees Ian jump the pole, he is confident to follow. Thankfully Ian keeps well to the side as Prince jumps. Throughout the exercise I was more worried about Ian being in danger than concentrating on the horse, but the method of the horse following a trusted friend has worked beautifully.

b

Yell and growl; again, say whatever you say to him when he's standing on your foot!

As soon as he stops reversing, stop smacking and kick like mad again. He must find the solution for himself. He knows that kick means move forwards and he knows that if he goes into reverse you will smack him again, and so let him choose the best option. You must be consistent. Do not get agitated when he won't budge because your kicking doesn't work immediately. Encouraging him to forwards from your stick is the wrong thing to do and all that previous kicking will be wasted.

Kick to go, smack if he reverses. The rule should be crystal clear to him and unless you establish this in his mind you are going to end up battling with him over everything you want him to do.

It is much easier to use a helper and so try to enlist a friend but make sure they know to skip well out of the way once they are over the jump.

Because Prince has responded so well and has not worked too hard, he is asked to tackle a tray with water in it for the first time (Figure 15.3). Again, Ian led the way and Prince followed him over the jump (Figures 15.4a and b).

Figure 15.3 Preparing for the next step with real water!

a

Figures 15.4a and **b** Same method, same result, and Ian is learning too. I am so relieved to see him out of Prince's way.

b

Once Prince was quite happy to pop over the water tray in the arena on his own (Figure 15.5), he was asked to do a different one out on the practice course. Here in the new surroundings, Ian was used again. It is much better to avoid a confrontation when things have started to go well (Figures 15.6a–c).

When a larger water tray is introduced, Prince soon finds his confidence to go it alone (Figure 15.7). It won't be much longer before Prince is confident enough to emulate Stewie (Figure 15.8).

A water tray need not be a hindrance to your horse's jumping. If you follow the steps that Angela has used with Prince, you will encourage, not force, your young horse to cooperate, even if he doesn't care for the jump. The only element in question is the time that it will take to be successful. As long as you build his confidence up gradually and make sure he is relaxed and happy with the combination of tray and poles you are using before you ask any more, you should be able to overcome any fears or

Figure 15.5 Prince is now happy on his own.

opposite page
Figures 15.6a–c Once again, the same methods were used achieving the same good result. All three of them did really well.

opposite page
left **Figure 15.7** Prince has got his confidence now and pops straight over this larger water tray with no lead from Ian.

right **Figure 15.8** Stewie and Mary; this is as good as it gets!

a

b

c

spookiness (Figure 15.9). The same methods will work just as well with a horse or rider who has had bad experiences with water jumps; just take it slowly and methodically. You might even feel better starting off with a blue painted plank as little as a foot wide to step over. Just don't take no for an answer, it is only one little step, but be prepared to take all the time you need to cajole and persuade rather than bully.

Triple bars

Q *I hate the look of a triple bar, how can I become more confident with it?*

A *Approach it with a positive attitude, analyse the jump instead of viewing it as a problem and practise jumping it as often as possible.*

The triple bar or staircase type of jump will usually only appear once on a course, if at all, and so consequently many riders don't see it very often. If you walk the course and immediately focus on any particular jump that you don't like the look of, you can guarantee that you will be anxious about doing well over it, and your horse will immediately pick up on your thoughts.

A triple bar or staircase jump can be a real rider stopper. It may look very imposing as obviously it will be wider than a normal parallel. It is almost irresistible to pace the width of a triple bar when you walk the course. Your eyes will be drawn to the spread and you won't like it. A nappy rider? The right sort of practice will stop you worrying about it and it will become very straightforward. Because the front element is always very low in comparison to the actual height of the back pole, you can discount it except as a take-off guide. The only time you are likely to knock a front pole off is if you are looking down and dropping your hands instead of concentrating on your rhythm and impulsion.

Figure 15.9 Prince is proving that all Ian's hard work has paid off as he pops straight over the water jump on show day. He might be a little spooked, but he is jumping it. As long as Angela has enough leg on, the spookiness can work for her because it encourages Prince to jump higher, just to make sure!

If you analyse the jump instead of looking at it warily you will see that if the final element was just a plain upright, your ideal take-off point would be where you should be taking off for the triple bar. The first two poles of the spread are really irrelevant, and only make the jump look more imposing than it really is. If you look for a take-off point at the usual distance from the first low pole, you are going to be a very long way off the back pole. However hard it may be, you must get it into your head that the low poles on this staircase jump don't matter, they might just as well not be there – except for the fact that they put you off! The obvious solution to riding this jump better is to get more practice over it, and there is a grid that will help you develop the right attitude and confidence to deal with something you simply don't like the look of.

You will already be familiar with a 7-cross grid at bounce distances and so Step 1 is to work through that a few times. For Step 2 change the grid so that the jumps at either end are ascending parallels both in and out, with an upright left in the middle. Ascending parallels, unlike true parallels, have the back pole higher than the front pole.

You can see from Diagram 17 that when you build up to Step 3, the spare wings are positioned on the inside of the last jump to make an additional cross pole so making the distance for the non-jumping stride 0.6 m (2 ft) shorter. The original last ascending parallel is left at the same height and the ends of the additional cross should be the same height as the back pole of the spread (see photos 15.10a and b).

> **Note** *Never* jump or set a parallel when the back pole is lower than the front as it would be unfair to the horse. He would not be able to judge the effort needed if the back pole wasn't clearly observed or defined.

Boris and **Julie**

Julie and Boris event, and Boris just needs some practice at this sort of fence to discourage him from doing an unnecessarily massive leap. If Julie judges her take-off point at the normal 0.9–1.2 m (3–4 ft) in front of the low poles, it makes the actual back pole a very long way off. If she jumps it trying to focus purely on the far pole, she will minimize the spread and Boris won't have to stretch. As stated, the lower poles can be ignored.

Julie has a tendency to be protective of Boris who is still very much a novice, and she will find that producing a short and bouncy stride will be very effective. This is not easy with Boris being so big, but well worth the effort for the show-jumping phase. The 7-cross bounces got them both in the right mode and he found the change to the combination at Step 2 very easy.

When the two pairs of wings of the third jump were set at 7.3 m (24 ft), Boris had no difficulty whatsoever in coping with the distance and spread, and Julie did not find it intimidating. By positioning the third pair of wings with the cross on the inside of the last jump, leaving the non-jumping distance at 6.7 m (22 ft), Boris really didn't need to stretch any further. The very nature of this staircase jump on the grid means that the horse can practise taking off much closer than normal to the front poles of the last jump. The first part can be ignored. Because the extra spread of the jump is built with low ascending poles, it must really be discounted as having any influence over the way that Boris jumps it. He should take off in exactly the same place as he had already been doing on the previous conventional jump. The only negative influence for Boris would be Julie not really liking the look of it, and he would be able to sense that. (Figures 15.10a and b)

Diagram 17 Grid for building confidence with triple bars

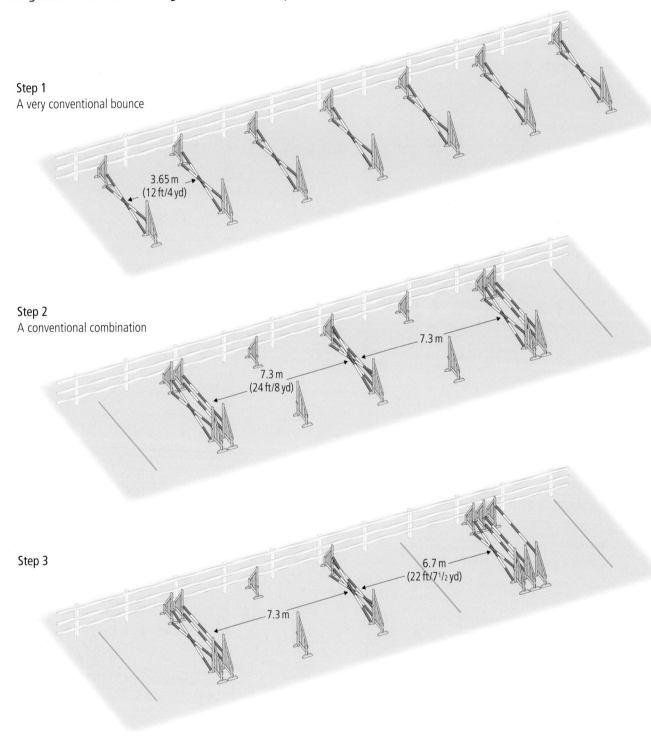

Step 1
A very conventional bounce

3.65 m
(12 ft/4 yd)

Step 2
A conventional combination

7.3 m

7.3 m
(24 ft/8 yd)

Step 3

6.7 m
(22 ft/7½ yd)

7.3 m

If you want to get this exercise into perspective, prove to yourself that it is not too imposing by initially jumping just an upright positioned on the furthest pair of wings and then go back and look at your horse's footprints. You will find that the position from which he took off would have enabled him to clear the spread of all three parts of the fence had the poles been in place.

You should jump this triple bar on the grid several times until you start to feel more comfortable with it. It shouldn't feel any different to any other jump, but you must work very hard at looking up because those low poles are a terrible draw, they seem to beckon your eyes downwards (Figure 15.11). You will not then like the look of the spread, your horse will immediately realize you don't like it, and he won't like it either.

As with the other grids, not only will this grid give you confidence with triple bars but will also boost your confidence generally (Figure 15.12).

a

above and below **Figures 15.10a** and **b** Julie and Boris have worked through all the suggested grid sequences to get to this point and she has made it very easy for Boris. You can see how effortless it is for him to make the spread.

b

left **Figure 15.11** After the reassuring practice on the grid, Julie tries hard not to look down at the triple bar, the practice course jump number 3, and Boris makes a very confident jump.

Figure 15.12 The grid and the jumping practice has given Julie the confidence to be a little more demanding with Boris's canter. He is normally very smooth and fractionally lazy, and so the bouncy shorter stride she asks him for suits the whole practice course, not just the triple bar. She is looking well ahead and is ready to gather him up and ride the two-stride double, fence 5, very positively in this jump-off practice.

Stiles

 Why do I always knock a stile down?

 You don't have to, it isn't compulsory, but stiles are difficult to jump well. As with most disliked fences, it is the appearance that puts the rider off.

Riders are well aware that with stiles they need to steer a bit more accurately; it is easier for a horse to run out at a stile purely because there isn't a lot of jump to point them at. If you ride a poor line or a wiggly slalom approach to an ordinary-width jump, you stand far more chance of jumping it, even if you are off centre. You have a bit of leeway, which you do not have with a stile, there simply isn't room to allow for a poorly steered approach, and most horses are far too clever to rub the wing. They might rub your leg on the wing, but their instincts to protect themselves will usually keep them safe.

A stile can be made more or less difficult by its position. If it is against the fence or abuts another jump, you should find it easier to ride a good line, but if it is out on its own, an island fence, you will have to shape up and be very positive about telling your horse exactly what you want.

CJ and **Shelly**

The stile on the practice course had a jump on its left, but this didn't prevent CJ running left and actually jumping through the gap between the wings, most uncomfortable for Shelly. Because he had cut in on the approach and then gone across the jump, a ground pole strategically placed to help the steering enabled Shelly to jump in the middle (Figures 15.13a and b).

Figures 15.13a and b
The ground pole helped Shelly make a square approach to the fence and she stayed very focused giving CJ no option other than to jump straight in the middle.

a

b

If you find it difficult to steer into a narrow jump, practise first with two ground poles like the ones used on the stay-straight exercises (see Chapter 5). They will guide you to guide your horse but don't rely on them for long; just let them help you begin to develop a better steering technique. The main thing that will help you improve your jumping of stiles is to look where you want to go and stay focused on this route. If you use a little more leg on your approach but don't let the horse go any faster, your hands should have a slightly stronger contact and so more control of the steering. Point your knuckles at the middle of the jump and try to do it far enough away – three or four strides – so that you don't want to change your mind as you get closer. Be consistent and keep your leg on so that your horse has plenty of confidence and stays straight as he faces a narrow aperture.

Try to pretend the jump is of normal width, as an overcautious approach will make things worse.

There is another reason, a practical reason, why a stile will fall more often than a normal-width jump, even if you approach it in the middle. Stile poles are only half the length of an ordinary pole and only half the weight, and so it doesn't take such a strong rub or knock to dislodge them. The answer is, of course, not to rub the pole, and you can use the method that Shelly uses with CJ if he becomes a little casual or slovenly (see page 181).

It all comes back to schooling or practising in the right manner and with the right attitude. The more you practise your steering and impulsion with a narrow obstacle, the easier it will be to jump it better, and you should reach the stage where you don't allow yourself to ride it differently from any other jump.

'You needn't think I'm jumping that!'

A lady rider used to come to me for training on her own horse, ride into the arena, scan the jumps, pick one out and say, 'You needn't think I'm jumping that!'

The year before, this lady's catch phrase was, 'Well I'll give it a go'. One or two bad experiences plus some time away from riding had brought about a serious loss of confidence and we were all three struggling to recapture her previous form and attitude.

It might have been a stile or a tray, a triple bar or a combination, but she was very ready to nap, long before her horse did. And of course, with that in her head, she was always going to mess it up, almost to prove herself right. The jump she chose certainly wouldn't have been higher or wider than any of the others on the practice course, but if she didn't like

the look of it that was that; there could be no discussion.

Eventually loads of confidence-building grid work, and even more importantly help from a hypnotist, sorted her out; now she events and will tackle anything in front of her with no hesitation.

A hypnotist or possibly a sports psychologist can do as much, or more, than a trainer to instil confidence. The trainer can work on the physical aspects, but if the rider slips back to square one between sessions, it does present a problem. Repetitive grid work was very valuable, but to make any progress over ordinary fences this particular lady rider had to be encouraged severely, almost bullied, to get on with it, and that's not how I like to train. Although we always did as much as I hoped to in each training session, it usually involved some backtracking and lowering the particular hated fence and then building it up again gradually. And it happened every time.

Then, one day she came for a training session and resisted nothing, she jumped everything first time with no hesitation. I couldn't help but remark on her attitude and that's when she told me she'd seen a hypnotist. What an improvement in her jumping! The horse picked up on her new confidence and flew round instead of being beset by doubts, and so far they haven't looked back. But perhaps the story is best told in this rider's own words.

'The problem with confidence – or the lack of it – is that it's all in your mind until it travels down your reins! With me it started with height – it had to be less than three foot. Then it got to be anything a bit "skinny", or a parallel that was a bit too wide – every time I went for a lesson I'd look for a problem fence that I couldn't possibly even attempt. Needless to say I was jumping it by the end of the lesson, but the next time would be just the same, albeit with a different fence. Poor Carol used all her skills just to get me back to where I was the last time I left her!

'It was a chum who wanted to give up smoking that set me thinking – she'd been hypnotized into quitting and it had worked; "its all in the mind" she had been told and that rang a bell! Despite being a bit of a cynic, I was getting so frustrated at not being able to tackle the courses that I wanted to jump, and knew that I was capable of, that I went to see a hypnotist who knew absolutely nothing about horses and even less about jumping.

'It seemed very peculiar to be telling a complete stranger that you were perfectly capable of doing something physically but you just couldn't bring yourself to do it, particularly when they had no background with horses and had never experienced this problem themselves.

'I can't say that I felt any real difference in myself afterwards, but the next time I went to Carol's we were both pleasantly surprised that she didn't have to spend the whole lesson trying to convince me that I could still jump a fence that I'd done only a week before. She didn't have to take the back rails off parallels and I didn't refuse to jump anything that looked a bit "scary".

'I have no idea how or why this worked, it may be something about the state of hypnosis or it may be that the hypnotist knew nothing about horses. When we tell other horsy people of our fears about a particular fence they normally sympathize; most people have a "bogey" fence and can understand the feeling, whereas a non-horsy person probably thinks that you can either jump or not in the same way that you can either sing or not.

'I went to several sessions and Carol is now able to get back to improving my jumping rather than having to convince me that I can do it at all. It may not work for everyone but it certainly helped me.'

The next time I encounter anyone with a similar anxiety, I will put her in touch with my lady rider to discuss her methods of regaining confidence. It has made training her a pleasure once more.

16 Pre-show practice

Grid work has become a straightforward routine, your figure-of-eight grids are proficient, your steering is positive and accurate, and you rarely touch a pole. You are jumping better. You now, therefore, should decide whether you want to be competitive and go further and present your skills in public.

In Chapters 18 and 19 I discuss the various options available for you and your horse, either BSJA classes, Trailblazers, or maybe you would prefer local unaffiliated show jumping, and so it should be simple to choose the level you wish to take part in.

It would be sensible to make sure you are happy and confident with jumping round a slightly bigger course in practice than the size of course you plan to start competing over. Arriving at the show and walking a daunting course will not help you do your best and jump better. If you aren't confident, your nerves will kick in and you will jump worse than usual.

Choose your show venue wisely. A show that uses a recognized or qualified course builder would be best as he will know the standards and distances required to get the right result. He would be aiming to get about one in five competitors jumping clear in the first round, and to set a jump-off round which rewards the most proficient and clean jumping partnership. He is unlikely to build what I would classify as an unfair track, as his expertise should allow him to get plenty of four-fault rounds

without one particular bogey fence or line being the cause. Difficult is acceptable, tricky is not.

Trying to improve your jumping over a tricky or trappy course with awkward related distances is not going to be easy if you are an inexperienced rider or have a novice horse, and you would be better off not entering. If there is a huge entry, particularly in the early novice classes, obviously the show organizers need to get the classes moving on, but building an unfair track to sort competitors out should not be the way to make up time. Judge if the course is trappy or not by walking it carefully and hope that it presents no surprises. The jumps should follow on in some sort of logical sequence: number 2 should be easily accessible from number 1 and so on. If you are surprised at the direction and line you are expected to take or if you have to hunt to find the next number, it is probably not the right course for you to start with. Of course you should expect to find doglegs and diagonal approaches, you have practised all that at home, but not from an awkward corner where you can't maintain your impulsion.

Do you have to put the brakes on to negotiate a turn? Are the distances surprisingly short or extra long in the doubles or combinations? I've walked courses where one side of the double has been a yard shorter than the other, giving an offset appearance, or the distance has left me wondering just how many half strides the course builder was hoping to produce. If the course is obviously built to penalize you for riding consistently and well, have the strength of mind to leave well alone till another day and a better track.

A difficult track is entirely different from an unfair one and if you recognize any areas where you must be extra positive with your presentation, approaches and impulsion, the horse should find the track as simple as the work you do at home.

A course that has the first fence sited to be jumped away from the collecting ring or the last fence just round the corner from, and at right angles to, the exit, is difficult but not unfair. You are going to have to be very positive just to get started and finish well. A sharp dogleg needs positive steering and it is something you should already have practised at home with your figure-of-eight or fan grids. Diagonal lines must be well ridden and the horse should not be surprised about where he's asked to go, it is up to the rider to let him know in time, not throw him round a corner at the last second with no time to prepare to jump.

There are only so many variations a course builder can include on his track and if the related distances are conventional, you should be able to cope with anything he throws at you, especially if you have used the right practice methods at home or when schooling.

A BSJA course designer builds a new course for me every two weeks or so. My riders jump it as set for the first week, I turn it round to be jumped a different way for the next week and then the course builder comes again. For my riders, it is a perfect arrangement as they get to jump the sort of courses he is setting at shows. I would soon get in a rut with building my own practice courses because it is very tempting to build too easy and straightforward tracks that I know the riders can do well, especially when I am trying to encourage them. But I don't want the riders to get to a show knowing that they are perfectly capable of jumping the size of the fences set in the schedule, and then be surprised

by the severity of the track or route they are meant to negotiate.

If you don't have these sorts of facilities, try to access a course to practise over; most of the show centres hire out their arenas between shows and so do take advantage of this before you go to a competition. It will be particularly helpful if you can do this directly after the centre has run the type of show you hope to enter as it will give you some idea of the layout of track that a particular course builder favours. If you find his turns or distances difficult, then you should do a little more homework first. It is all about preparation, leaving nothing to chance, and if there is anything you can organize to help you jump better on the day, make sure you do it.

The course plan shown is ideal for a pre-show schooling session (Diagram 18). It includes just about everything required to practise over before venturing into competition. There are both left-handed and right-handed dogleg approaches, related distances in a straight line, a double with a parallel in on the left rein, and a treble combination with an upright in from the right rein with one- and two-stride distances to a parallel out. There is a water tray, a narrow stile, a triple bar, and all are brightly coloured. If you have the course set slightly larger than you intend to tackle at your show and jump round this course nice and smoothly, you should be ready for anything you might find when you take your horse out to compete.

It is a good idea to walk the course on foot before you jump it, especially if you can discuss with your trainer the methods and technique required to jump well. It will also put into perspective the size of the fences and make you aware of not being too ambitious as far as size is concerned when you plan to enter a competition. If 0.84 m (2 ft 9 in) looks big to you when you walk it when you're schooling, it will look even bigger when you walk the course at a show. Don't be afraid to be

Centre: **FOXES CLOSE**   Date: 3rd May 2007

Course Designed by: KEITH DELLAR (BSJA Median Course Designer (55325)

(Teaching/Training Course designed to BSJA standards)

First Round: Fences: 1, 2, 3ABC, 4, 5, 6AB, 7, 8, 9	Jump Off: 1-2-9 (reversed)-5-6AB-7 Fences: (or) 5-6AB-2-9 (rev)-8 (rev)-1
Optional Two Phase: First Phase Fences: 1, 2, 3ABC, 4, 5, 6AB, 7	Second Phase: Fences: 8, 9, 2 (rev), 5, 6AB, 4 (rev)

Diagram 18 Foxes Close course plan

sensible. If you walk the same course after you have jumped it, you will find it looks much less intimidating. It is all a question of perspective and confidence. You will feel so much more at ease about jumping well if you know you have been jumping a bigger track at home.

Once you are consistently jumping double clear rounds, it is then time to move up a step, not before, however much well-meaning friends try to encourage you to be bolder. Certainly, you might need a nudge to move on and up when you are ready, but let the trainer advise you on this.

If you aren't a professional show jumper or eventer there is no reason why you shouldn't try to ride like one. Maybe you don't have a string of horses, but you can concentrate on the one you do have and prepare him just as carefully as the top riders prepare their horses. Although you don't have to win a class to make a living, it is always satisfying to do as good a job as possible, and if you leave nothing to chance, the results should speak for themselves. Don't be

casual when you are practising; have a proper dress rehearsal, treat the schooling session like a show, and don't expect your horse to read your mind because you are only schooling. If you save a posh pair of boots just for shows, both for you and the horse, make sure you wear them for this practice, even if it means extra washing and polishing! If you use a different hat or carry a smarter stick, make sure you also use them for practice. If you want to use spurs at the show, you must use them at home too. Play a radio when you are working to get him used to loudspeakers. Anything unfamiliar on show day could be a distraction for both of you, and all this extra attention to little details will pay dividends. Try very hard to establish a warm-up routine at home, and use the same routine every time, then when you use that same routine at a show, it will give you both the confidence to work as well as you know you can (Figure 16.1).

If I were walking this course, either as rider or trainer, these would be my tactics. Before you

Figure 16.1 Although you won't be able to use grid work at a show, have a good warm up before jumping the practice course. If a show is imminent, then work over your warm up routine at the practice so your horse knows what to expect.

commence your round, trot or canter round the arena in a low-key manner and get your bearings. Once the bell goes, check, go down to walk or trot and *then* start your working, up-tempo jumping canter, the one you've been practising so hard to establish. Remember, always check, slow down, and *then* increase the power and get on with the job. If the horse before you has had several knockdowns, you could be circling and waiting for several minutes while the course is reset. The canter will inevitably deteriorate and if when you hear the bell you just canter to the first fence in the same type of canter and frame of mind, your horse will not realize that you mean to start. You don't want to be circling on full power while you wait for the bell if it is going to be a long wait. Practise this aspect of ring craft, and establish the method and signal you will give the horse to start every time you practise. A tap on the shoulder or your boot, a click or a vocal warning, whichever signal you use, use it *every* time without fail. You owe it to your horse to make it crystal clear when you point him at the first fence and expect him to switch on to jumping mode. It is so demoralizing to have a refusal or knockdown at the first fence because your horse is simply ill prepared.

Riding the Foxes Close course

Frankie and Diane are getting ready for the BSJA British Novice Regional Finals and are practising over the Foxes Close course. I've awarded the jumps on the course with marks out of 10 for difficulty, 10 being the most demanding, and the jump numbers in the text below tally with the jump numbers on Diagram 18.

Number 1 (Figure 16.2)is away from the exit and placed on the diagonal; you must, therefore, be very positive to avoid him hanging towards the gate or comfort zone and very accurate with your steering. You should circle round on the left rein before you

start, well away from and behind the first jump, *never* in front of it. If you circle in front of the first fence before you mean to jump it, you may have a misunderstanding with him about your intentions when you do want him to jump it, even if you give him your signal to start. There is no necessity for there to be any confusion, so don't allow it to happen.

As soon as you are ready, with your strong jumping canter established, straighten up for your approach, and signal to your horse to make sure he understands that this is the first jump. As discussed, this understanding should already have been worked out between you to ensure that he knows what you mean but maybe you should use a little more leg, without going faster, to push the horse round the corner and away from the exit. Beware of overshooting your turn and make sure as you jump that you have your eye on number 2. **Jump 1 – 7/10.**

Number 2 (Figure 16.3) is approached on the right-hand dogleg, and you have plenty of room to straighten up if you look where you are going. This approach should remind you of the work you have been doing on the figure-of-eight grids. **Jump 2 – 5/10.**

Just remember you would need to land with a strong outside rein to prevent your horse cutting in round the corner to the combination at fence number 3 (Figure 16.4). He wouldn't be naughty or nappy as he thinks he knows where he's going and wants to anticipate the turn, but you must be on guard to stop him doing it. You want maximum revs as you come off the corner to approach number 3 so use lots of inside leg into a very supportive outside rein. If you let him cut the corner, the inside hind leg won't be as strong and pushy, and so as you straighten up don't ease the outside rein forward to help your steering. Keep nudging him into that outside support to ensure you can tackle number 3 with loads of impulsion and energy, not speed.

Figure 16.2 Number 1: good stride off the diagonal to the first fence. Diane might well be pleased with this approach.

Figure 16.3 Frankie jumps well but slightly to his left. He has been a bit keen across the related distance and made up a little too much ground, and so he has gone a little wider and off centre at jump number 2 to give himself a touch more room on takeoff. Diane is looking round the corner to the next line.

Number 3 is a combination built with an upright in and a conventional 7.5 m (24 ft 6 in) single stride to another upright, then two strides to the final element of a true parallel at a 10.7 m (35 ft) distance. This would not, therefore, present any surprises. The siting along the fence and heading towards home encourages the horse to keep going and stay straight. The ordinary grid work you have done from the very beginning should make this uncomplicated, and the only thing you should remember is not to motor on to the last element. It would be very easy to tip the front pole if your horse is moving on and you are too far forward over his shoulder as he is coming up in front. **Jump 3 – 6/10.**

Again, think about your outside rein as you land so that you can push and steer round the more difficult turn to jump number 4 (Figure 16.5). Don't forget to turn your head so that your horse gets an early warning signal about where you want him to go. If you ride round the corner in dressage mode, looking between his ears, you might find that when you do turn, the jump isn't quite where you expected it to be. Also, you don't want him to think you are jumping number 8.

Number 4 (Figure 16.6) is a simple upright, but is jumped off the diagonal directly away from the gate.

If you have enough outside rein after the combination and hold and push your horse out round the turn, the approach to 4 should have plenty of energy. If you let him cut in, you are going to be too short of space to get a good shot off the corner. **Jump 4 – the jump itself is 4/10, but the approach and position makes it 7/10.**

Number 5 comes up rather quickly and so make sure as you jump 4 you are looking where you are

Figure 16.4 Frankie makes a good job of 'pinging', jumping with lots of spring and energy, through the combination but still with a slight tendency to jump to the left.

Figure 16.5 Because Frankie is so pleased with his efforts and knows where he's going, Diane has her work cut out to stop him motorbiking round the corner.

meant to be going next. When you land, push on immediately as the related distance of five strides works well if you keep going in your strong rhythm. If you are not positive with your steering and go too wide or cut in, you will arrive on an uncomfortable stride and make this particular jump awkward for your horse; your steering needs to be spot on.

Number 5 as a parallel should be a bit of a breather fence, or it would be if you weren't being asked to jump diagonal poles (Figure 16.7). Jump it in the middle because any deviation with the steering could make you rattle a pole and, again, be ready to land and prevent the horse anticipating the turn to jump numbers 6 and 7. **Jump 5 – 5/10.**

Moving from jump 5 round to 6 and 7, you need to ride a very positive three-quarter turn. If you cut in, you can't hope to get a strong and straight approach across the diagonal. As soon as you've

landed after 5, hang on to the outside rein and push your horse round the corner. Again, it is a skill you should have established from practising the figure-of-eight grids.

Number 6 is a one-stride double, with a parallel in and an upright out, and will be very straight-forward if your steering is good (Figure 16.8). There is no fence to guide you in and so you must rely on turning your head at the right time in order to see where you have to go. Remember, your horse picks up on this movement from your head and is on alert for the steering aid which comes fractionally afterwards. If you ride this left turn as positively as you rode the right turn round to number 4, you should be square on for both parts of the double and, most importantly, the related distance on a straight line to the triple bar at number 7. You mustn't turn too early for the first part of the

above **Figure 16.6** Diane is preparing well for the short dogleg to jump number 5.

right **Figure 16.7** This is a lovely effort at these asymmetric poles; Diane must have ridden a good line, and she is still enjoying herself.

double because you must hold your horse out round the turn long enough so that you are lining up for the middle of the second part too. It is so easy to cut in to the first jump and not get in line for the second part, which will make the distance longer, maybe too long, and actively encourage a run out or refusal. **Jump 6 – double rating 6/10; approach 8/10.**

Jump number 7 (Figures 16.9a and b) should be a 4/10, but only if you have landed straight after the double and maintained the rhythm and impulsion necessary to arrive at this wider jump on a comfortable four-stride approach. It could be rated as high as a 7/10 if you don't jump the double well and if you relax, meddle with the steering, and don't keep up the energy and power across the four-stride related distance. Just think, too, that your horse will be in the air over this particular jump perhaps a little longer than you anticipate because it is wider, so don't shift your weight to land too soon and make him drop a toe on the back pole. **Jump 7 – from 4/10 to 7/10**

You have plenty of room for the turn into fence number 8 but this is a spooky fence for some horses because of the water tray beneath the upright poles, and so you must not relax coming round the corner away from the exit gate (Figure 16.10). And you *are* coming directly away from this gate, so be on guard for any hint of reluctance. When a horse jumps a demanding line well, like 6 across to 7, there is a tendency for the rider to relax very slightly, and it is possible that the horse might think he has finished; it will, therefore, come as a surprise when the rider gears up for another jump.

The horse doesn't even have to be nappy to slow down or hang to the exit, just a little bias in that direction is enough to cause a slight loss of power and commitment. This is why I try to do the initial grid work away from the exit gate, so that the horse understands that the gate is not a comfort zone. Stay alert yourself; if you are consistent, the horse should keep going in the same manner and therefore you must make sure that you are thinking 'work' all the way round the course to the finish.

Figure 16.8 This green double on one stride, followed by four strides to the triple bar, must look a right jumble of poles to Frankie. Diane has ridden a good unhurried line round the corner and waited to give him time and room to look and assess what he has to do next.

a

b

As a simple upright of poles this fence would rate a 4/10 if it weren't for the water tray underneath it. If your horse doesn't like it, it could well be 10/10 for you! Just remember that even an experienced horse can sometimes play up at a water tray, especially if you have been too relaxed and the fence comes up as a bit of a surprise to him. In Chapter 15 I explained a method of encouraging the reluctant horse to go straight over a tray and so make sure you have given him every opportunity to be very confident, and hopefully even blasé, when he sees water. **Jump 8 – from 4/10 to 10/10.**

Jump number 9 is a stile, a narrow jump that will require your steering to be very accurate, but don't approach it too cautiously and be too careful. Try to ride it as if it were a normal-width fence, otherwise your horse will pick up your hesitation and wonder what is wrong. The approach to this jump should be ridden very positively. Your horse might look at number 2, but not if you turn your head to look at number 9 in time. Let him know where you want him to go by committing your eye to the middle of the jump and your horse will get it right too. Avoid cutting in too soon in order to avoid heading towards number 2 because the slant approach to a narrow fence can end in disaster with

Figures 16.9a and **b** a) Diane has held Frankie slightly to the left over the fence as she knows what he is going to try next; he is already very slightly on the slant. Note how Diane is counteracting this by keeping her inside shoulder up and hanging on to the new outside rein.
b) Despite Diane's best efforts Frankie still tries to nip round the corner in his own way. She really has to argue with him to try to keep him from cutting the corner round to the next fence.

below **Figure 16.10** Diane is delighted to have won the argument with Frankie to present him fair and square to the water tray.

a stop or run out. Obviously a stile will knock down more easily than a long pole as it is only half the weight, but it won't knock down if you don't touch it! Try not to be too sensitive and do treat it as an ordinary obstacle. I would be more concerned about knocking it down because it is the last fence rather than because it is narrow (Figure 16.11).

Jump 9 – 8/10.

Last-fence-jockey syndrome

How many times have I heard 'we were going so well and I just tipped the last fence'? Too many times! It is human nature to relax after a job well done, but if you relax too soon, you will spoil your

round. When riders are practising the course, they don't seem able to prevent themselves collapsing at the last jump, however many times they are warned about going through the finish before they start to feel pleased. When I'm training people, I shout so many times before the last jump, 'don't spoil it now!', but it seems that when they aren't reminded, they can't help relaxing that split second too soon.

If the rider relaxes and collapses on take off at this last obstacle and goes forward too early, the consistency of contact that the horse has felt during the whole of the round is lost and so he won't stay tidy in front. Even when a rider has waited, got the horse off the ground perfectly and the horse has really snapped his front legs up, they get over the top of the fence, say 'Good boy', relax and drop the contact and sit down too early, inviting the horse to drop his hind legs anticipating the landing too.

You must drill yourself into imagining you have another fence to jump afterwards, and try to ride accordingly. It is such a disappointment when the fault is entirely yours and very avoidable.

Course practice

You will notice that most of my advice concerns the parts of the course in between the fences. If you've done your grid work well enough, only the appearance of the fences will prevent you jumping them well, and your horse can soon be encouraged to get over that by practising different types of obstacles. I don't worry about the size or nature of the jumps, only the method of presentation and approach. It is only at the first jump that you have time to

Figure 16.11 Diane takes the last fence in fine style, no chance of being a last-fence jockey, she keeps her weight well in the stirrups so that Frankie's back end is well clear of the pole. Diane might well look pleased with such a nice round.

establish the right sort of canter, and you need so much concentration and consistency to land and pick up that canter immediately after every fence, particularly when your horse knows where he is going and tries to dive off round the corners prematurely. Nor is it helpful if he is too keen and rushes his related distances or is decidedly lazy and wants to pop in extra strides when there isn't really room.

The only way you are going to ride your courses better is by practising them under the right conditions, i.e. over a track. The grids have given you all the skills you need to make a good job of your consistency and steering, but you need to put them into practice round a whole course of nine or ten fences. Get that organized and jumping better will be a foregone conclusion (Figure 16.12).

Figure 16.12 Show day. Frankie flying over the first with Diane ready for the sharp left jump-off turn.

17 Show preparation and good manners

There are one or two other considerations that will certainly help you be less stressed and jump better when you go to a show: sensible preparation and good manners.

The preparation should be thorough and a routine established so that when you get to the show, you don't find you have forgotten something: girth, bridle, martingale, stirrups, studs, boots, hat, stick, your boots, or money. Riders have turned up for training minus one or more of their essentials and usually I have been able to lend or substitute the forgotten items. But what a mess you would be in at a show, especially if you did not know anyone there who would be able to help you out.

If you are going to a strange place, get your route properly sorted out the day before, you don't want to be stuck somewhere having to resort to telephoning for directions miles from the venue.

Late arrival can sometimes be unavoidable if the traffic has been bad, but not leaving early enough to arrive in time to walk the course for your class is careless and lazy. I was at a show when a well-known rider turned up with four horses right at the tail end of the class in which he wanted to ride. Because he was who he was, the executive allowed him to enter and the whole competition was held up as he warmed up each horse individually to ride in the class. He was obviously too thick skinned to care about the other forty or so competitors who had to wait an extra hour before the jump off could

start. This demonstrates very bad manners, no matter how well known a rider is.

Forgotten kit or a late start, either of these is enough to distract you when you need to be calm and focused. Tacking up in a panic and warming up hastily is not going to encourage better jumping, however experienced you are; it is better to wait than be too late.

When you are at a show, whether competing, helping a rider, or just spectating, do you deplore some of the behaviour you observe? Do you feel that some of the competitors are ill-mannered, selfish and unhelpful, both to their fellow competitors and the officials who are helping to run the show? How do you imagine these officials feel about the very same behaviour? Remember, the officials give their time and effort willingly for no set fees. They aren't there to thwart your efforts but to encourage you to jump better by ensuring the show runs smoothly. The show can't run without judges, a secretary, a course builder and collecting ring stewards, plus the pole picker-uppers.

If you have just a minor falling out with any of them you won't jump well, and if you fall out badly, you may not even be allowed to jump at all. Just be prepared: have your entries ready when you go to see the secretary, stay cool if there is a queue and walk the course in good time.

Concentrate as you walk the course, it will be your knowledge and expertise that will tell your horse where and how he should be going once you start to ride the course. Not only will you have to remember the track or route to be taken, all the work you have done with your related distances will be important if you want to jump a clear round. Hopefully the distances in double or treble combinations should be conventional, because of course that is what you have been practising. And you should have also practised pacing those distances on the grid on your own two feet to discover exactly what does or doesn't suit your horse. You need to know if the course builder has made the distance either a shade shorter or longer than normal, so you will know whether to try to steady a little more, or sooner, or push a bit more strongly with your leg.

The timing and consistent impulsion and rhythm is so important when riding a course, but then you should already have established on the grids how you should 'feel' and ride almost automatically in almost all situations. As you walk the course, try to plan the route you want to ride on your horse. A straight approach to your first fence is essential, although you don't want it to be too long a run. Look for a nice straight line, with no hanging or leaning, when the jumps are in line, and develop an awareness of how many strides the course builder plans between the jumps. Will it suit your horse's particular way of going? All your grid work has been geared to work on that consistent stride, so plan to produce it all the way round, and remember to keep it up on the corners.

Make sure that you are aware of any dogleg approaches. This should not be too difficult for you as you have been practising looking where you are going on the figure-of-eight grid. You should also have practised riding to the middle of the next jump, and not slowing your horse beforehand to see where you need to go next. Every time you turn, plan to make sure you are pushing into that outside rein, and then *do not* ease it too far forward to help steer round the corner. You need to come off a

corner with the same amount of impulsion that your horse had before the turn. Both your straight and figure-of-eight grids will have helped you manage that.

Before you leave the ring, mentally review your plans until you are sure you've not overlooked any difficult approaches or lines, and don't forget to acknowledge the course builder or any other officials in the ring. 'Good morning' isn't hard to say, and makes the atmosphere more pleasant. Don't complain loudly to anyone who listens that you think such and such a jump is unfair but if you *do* think that, very quietly and politely go and speak to the course builder. You can rest assured that if you do take a dislike to a jump that will be the one you make a hash of. If you really don't like something, then withdraw, but don't make a fuss, especially if everyone else finds the course acceptable.

It all comes down to confidence and to whether you've done your homework well enough to be untroubled by the jumps in your class. But don't be too relaxed, the course will still be a challenge, however straightforward you think it is. And if you find the first round easy, you can always show how much better you can do by employing your jump-off techniques.

The officials' point of view

One judge says that a particular problem she sees is the reluctance by the competitors to come into the ring, whether it is the first class of the day or the first class after a lunch break. It is particularly frustrating for a judge to rush around at home seeing to her own animals and driving maybe an hour to the show to be in the judge's box ready to start at 9 am, only to have no sign of a competitor ready to start by 9.20 am. Judges don't like to have to nag the competitors and it does not set a pleasant tone for the rest of the day if you have to start threatening to close the class. I have seen classes closed because the riders are so difficult to get into the ring and if hurried, they do jump badly. Then they blame everything and everybody else but themselves instead of recognizing their lack of preparation.

For example, competitors know they should put their numbers down on the board when they've walked the course, they know they are going to take part, and so why are they often so reluctant to record their intention?

Be very polite to the steward on the board, she won't be having an easy time (Figure 17.1). When she contacts the judges with the order of numbers, it is disheartening to know that there are perhaps 40 entries, but only half a dozen numbers on the board. It all holds up the proceedings, not only for the officials but also the competitors, who will find the day gets longer and more delayed.

It won't help your jumping if you are mooching about for ages waiting to get in the ring. Try to cooperate and be ready, calm and collected when your number is called. Experience should tell you how long you need to allow for warming up and so don't be too early or too late. If you are called too soon, you will be unhappy because your warm-up has been interrupted, if you are ready to go earlier than you are called, you might go off the boil. Try to judge your ring appearance accurately, if you get flustered in any way, your horse will pick up on it and be flustered too.

With less-experienced riders at unaffiliated shows, the judge is often in a position to offer a quick piece of advice to enable the competitor not to make the same mistake again, to actively try to

Figure 17.1 Don't crowd or harass the collecting ring steward, she has the power to be awkward if you upset her which won't help your performance.

help her jump better. At a recent show, a rider went through the start only to circle in front of the first jump, obviously with no intention of jumping it, but setting herself up to begin her round. It was only a clear-round class and so the judge kindly did not take the circle as a refusal. When the judge told her that the next time it happened, she would be penalized with a refusal, the rider did not take it in the manner the judge intended. She was not grateful at having her fault pointed out to her and was rather indignant to have been told she had been in the wrong.

She should have been pleased to discover why she had been in the wrong, because in a competitive class, she would most certainly have been awarded four faults, all before actually jumping a fence. Judges are not there to be difficult, they have a wealth of experience and have seen just about everything go wrong in the ring that can go wrong, and if they are kind enough to offer advice, take it.

In show jumping, the judge's decision is aided by a very clear rule book that sets out nearly every circumstance that might occur. There are lots of 'don'ts', to be taken notice of; let the common-sense rules help you to jump better. You won't do very well if you're disqualified and so make sure you're clear about the rules pertaining to either the clothes you wear or the tack you use.

Learn to conform to the rules and demonstrate good behaviour. Don't show yourself up with spoiled or petulant behaviour if things aren't going right because that definitely won't improve your riding. If your horse is behaving badly there's a great deal of difference between a couple of smacks for naughtiness and a severe beating. Don't be unfair to the horse, you will be bringing your sport into disrepute, and the judge will be quite justified in warning you about it.

The judges do not want to keep pulling riders up because they are not quite in compliance with the rule book; they want a trouble-free day with everyone enjoying themselves. They want to concentrate on the competition and obtain a result, not to have to check up on everyone to make sure they are conforming to the dress, tack and behaviour code.

If you let something upset you to the point of riding badly, maybe you should try harder to concentrate on your riding and improving yourself, rather than take too much notice of things you can't change.

Show tips

Here are some tips for jumping better at a show. If you follow them, pay attention to the details relevant to you, and don't get distracted by your own lack of preparation, or something aggravating you at the show itself, you'll do well, you'll jump better and better. Remember, if you don't like the course, it will be the same for everyone, so let them complain if they're not happy. Either get on with it or go home!

First round

1. Do your homework. Check the schedule and class times before you leave. Make sure you are well able to jump the size of class you enter easily.

2. Give yourself plenty of time to study and walk the course.

3. Don't get flustered in the practice ring.

4. Warm up to a routine you have established already at home, and be ready when the collecting ring steward calls you.

5. Establish a good rhythm and impulsion before you turn to the first fence.

6. Signal to your horse that you are about to start, especially if they have taken a long time before ringing the bell. Make sure you go through the start.

7. Don't cut corners to make your approaches unnecessarily difficult.

8. Be alert to the fact that your horse might have a bias towards the collecting ring, and be ready to ride positively past that area.

9. Don't relax as you take off at the last jump. It is so easy to have the last fence down because you have eased up on your riding too soon.

10. Make sure you go through the finish.

11. Don't use the horse as a grandstand, just because you can see more when you are higher up. He will appreciate your weight off him, especially if it is going to be a long day.

The jump-off

1. Don't turn into a different rider because time is now an important factor. Stay as cool as you were in the first round.

2. Concentrate on keeping the same balance, rhythm and impulsion that you had in the first round.

3. Plan to improve your time by taking fewer strides between fences, not going faster.

4. Practise jumping on the angle and short approaches to a fence at home. Then you will know just how much you can ask of your horse and get the right response.

5. Don't overdo the practice jumping, save it for the ring.

6. Check out any short turns you plan to try as you trot round before the bell goes. Have the confidence in yourself to plan your own route.

7. If you have a turn in mind, don't be put off because you see someone else try it and fail. You should know from your homework what your horse can or can't do successfully.

8. Remember to go through the start and finish, and don't be a last-fence jockey when you have gone well.

So, having plotted and planned the way to ride this course, what actually happens when you set out? Has the grid given you everything you need to do it well? Of course it has, but the tricky bit is remembering to reproduce the way of going and getting the steering accurate over unfamiliar obstacles.

18 The British Show Jumping Association (BSJA)

The BSJA is the governing body of show jumping in Great Britain and sets all the rules governing show jumping. It aims to improve and maintain standards of show jumping, and encourages members at all levels to compete over attractive and well-built courses. Even if shows are not affiliated to the BSJA, you will usually see in the schedules that the classes will be judged under BSJA guidelines.

One of my Q&A questions from *Your Horse* magazine was from a ten-year-old girl whose pony could jump 1.37 m (4 ft 6 in). She desperately wanted to know how she could compete at Olympia as she was sure her pony could do as well as anyone else. All I could do was explain that pony jumping wasn't on the schedule for Olympia, but that she must keep working at her jumping and I pointed her in the direction of the BSJA. If she turned out to be good enough, this little weekend pony rider could take that pony up through the grades and qualifying rounds and make it to the Horse of the Year Show. Perhaps she was another Pat Smythe, Liz Edgar, Caroline Bradley, or Ellen Whitaker in the making. The *only* thing that would stop her was not being good enough.

The BSJA has made sure the opportunities are there, and actively encourage potential competitors to try their hand and improve their show jumping. You don't have to have great ability and know-how to start with as, once you have gained confidence to progress with your show jumping, there are carefully structured levels of classes through which you may improve and advance your jumping. When you join the Association, the progress of you and your horse is monitored as the BSJA keeps on computer a permanent record of all the members and horses registered. You can obtain accurate details of the size, colour and winnings of any horse or pony registered with the BSJA on line. There is a discount for BSJA members and of course you can download your own horse's details free.

To compete at a BSJA show you must be a member of the Association riding a registered horse or pony. There are several different categories of membership, joining is easy, and forms are available from the head office at Stoneleigh. If you have any difficulties with the forms, the friendly BSJA staff in the office will be only too glad to help you. This membership will entitle you to the Rules and Year Book and the *British Show Jumping* magazine which is produced four times per year. The magazine covers a range of topics throughout the year featuring shows such as the Horse of the Year Show, the BSJA Festival of Show Jumping, Olympia and Hickstead combined with news on training, rule changes, breeding, the Association elections and of course features surrounding supplements, hard feeds, and even saddlery.

The membership fees for 2008 are listed below. You get a lot for your money, especially as insurance cover is also included.

Full jumping member	£113.00
Non-jumping member	£47.00
Associate member	£83.00
Junior associate member	£42.00
Junior member	£23.00

Q *Why should I join? What will the BSJA do for me?*

A *The BSJA itself gives 10 good reasons for joining the Association.*

The BSJA:

1. Provides classes for all ability levels.

2. Manages more than 2000 affiliated shows every year.

3. Encourages members of all standards and at all levels to enjoy fair competition over carefully prepared courses.

4. Provides a competition structure through which everyone can gradually progress, improving their own and their horses' performance and ability.

5. Provides free personal liability insurance.

6. Gives help, support and advice from your Area Representative.

7. Gives a free copy of the BSJA Rules and Year Book and free copies of the quarterly BSJA Magazine, *British Show Jumping*.

8. Offers a monthly Show Directory, published on the internet and updated.

9. Provides a friendly yet professional service.

10. Maintains national and regional training courses.

Q *Will I have to jump big courses to start with?*

A *No! The weekend rider can start with classes set at 0.8 m (2 ft 9 in) and the progressive nature of the competitions allows you to go as far as your ability will take you, right up to the Horse of the Year Show, Royal International Horse Show or Olympia.*

Because course sizes are so varied, you will only be limited by the ability of you and your horse. Qualified BSJA course builders design the courses, and the specific limits on size of each type of competition can be found in the rule book.

The BSJA has recently introduced a new category of shows at Intro level. These shows may start with one or two small unaffiliated classes, as small as the organizers wish, say at around 0.7 m (2 ft 3 in) or 0.8 m (2 ft 9 in). The maximum height allowed in this category of show is 1 m (3 ft 3 in), and the only winning restrictions for horses competing at these shows is when a British Novice qualifier is included in the schedule, which restricts entry to horses with winnings of less than £100 in total. This level of show will give you an easy introduction to the BSJA classes, and will encourage you to aim to improve and move on and up gradually if you wish without getting out of your depth, or not to move on or up at all. You will not be excluded from any of the

Intro classes because your horse has won too much prize money. Not everyone wants to leave their particular comfort-zone level of heights and now, to give every rider something to aim for, these Intro classes will award points for a Regional League as well as prize money. The BSJA will publish the League results so that riders can see how well they are doing. Even if they remain in the same classes and the size of the fences does not increase, the competition and rewards will still encourage the riders to jump better in order to move up the League Table. There is a big difference between a competent and consistent rider who usually does well, and a rider who just has a lucky win. The rider who works the hardest to jump better will usually come out on top, and it will be reflected and shown in the regular update of the League leaders.

There are three distinct groups who should welcome the new Intro category: novice horses, novice riders with more experienced horses and older or more experienced horses who need to lower their sights a little, for whatever reason.

Riders with novice horses will be able to compete over relatively small courses and allow their horses to gain confidence accordingly. There will be no pressure to move up to the next level until the rider feels the horse is doing well enough and is ready to tackle more demanding courses. The increase in height and difficulty is gradual and so moving on to the next level should not present too many problems if the horse has been prepared well.

The classes are also perfect for the novice rider wishing to gain experience without frightening himself but who owns a more experienced horse. The horse will not be excluded from this type of competition, even if he has already won too much money to stay in British Novice and Discovery classes, and his experience will help the rider get out of trouble if mistakes or misunderstandings happen.

The jumps won't be too big to cope with if a poor approach has left them in a muddle.

For many horses and riders the Intro schedule is a blessing because it caters for the horse who has done well in the past but who needs a drop in level to be able to continue jumping happily instead of being over-faced or having to retire. When a horse has been consistently jumping 1.1 m (3 ft 9 in) plus, or much higher, eventually he will reach the stage or an age when the smaller jumps will look far more inviting to him. It is sensible to give the horse an easier time in these smaller classes and so prolong his active and happy competition life. Because Intro classes place no entry restrictions on the amount a horse has won, they will give many horses who have reached their size limit in more advanced classes a new lease of life as they will be able to compete quite happily in what are in effect small open classes. The Intro classes are, therefore, good for the horse who can keep competing over decent courses in a more professional atmosphere and good for the rider with a more experienced horse who has reached the stage when he does not want to be over-faced but has won too much to stay in ordinary Novice classes.

There have been several instances of 'clocked' horses, i.e. horses who have reached their jumping limit but who have won too much to compete again in smaller classes. These horses have been renamed and re-registered. If the horse has been sold to a new owner who has no idea of what has gone on, this unwitting owner can still be disqualified if the deception is found out. The Intro category will help do away with the inclination to cheat in this way.

The only shows held before this innovation were more traditional shows (British Novice, Discovery, Newcomer and Foxhunter), now called Progressive level, which would have no classes with heights lower than the British Novice height of 0.9 m (3 ft). Once the horse had done well at that level and won

£100, the only option before the Intro shows would be to jump in Discovery classes, starting at 1 m (3 ft 3 in).

So many riders found this rather intimidating, especially as they can no longer enter British Novice classes first as a warm up. The unaffiliated early classes in the Intro category allows would-be members to compete in the affiliated environment with no extra expense and gives them a chance to make their minds up whether to join the BSJA or not. If they then want to have a go at an affiliated class without becoming a member first, they may buy a 'ticket to ride' option for the proper BSJA classes. This costs £6 plus the normal entry fees for the class and allows them to compete on equal terms with BSJA members. They won't receive any placing status, prize money or qualifications but it will give them a real chance to experience the BSJA courses first hand. They can test themselves to see if they are up to competing on level terms and compare their performance with members.

The traditional show falls into the BSJA Progressive category and will probably run its schedule starting with Novice classes and progressing upwards. The first-round maximum heights are set to be encouraging to both the inexperienced competitor and the novice horse, and no classes will have first-round fences higher than 1.1 m (3 ft 6 in).

The Advanced category show starts with heights no lower than 1.1 m (3 ft 6 in) and this level is something to aim for if your horse is talented and you want to take your jumping a bit more seriously. Don't be intimidated by the other competitors, even if they are international riders; the courses, heights and spreads are the same for everyone. You must plan to work harder to bring yourself up to scratch, to try to beat the course builder, not the other

riders, and to jump better and go clear.

If you are a weekend rider with only one horse, you can still do as well as more experienced riders if you do all the right things at home to enable you to go into the ring knowing your skills are in place. Have confidence in your training plans, do your grid work, do your figure-of-eight and jump-off-practice grids and learn how much you can ask from your horse. There is no need for your horse, however talented, to be over-faced or hurried at a show because you are too keen to get a good result. When training, you will also learn when it would be better to temper your ambitions and enthusiasm slightly, and make sure you are jumping cleanly in your jump-offs rather than being keen to the point of rushing and incurring knock-downs or glance-offs.

As well as organizing show jumping, the BSJA offers many fringe benefits to its members, the sort of packages you would normally expect from any good club. There are two-year discounted rates for Pony Club or BHS Riding Club members, a complete registration package for Junior Membership, and web access to horse or pony records. The show calendar can be checked out online and members can obtain horse and pony passports at Association rates.

The BSJA also have a list of Accredited Trainers who can assist you to improve your show jumping. You could join the 5-star training scheme if competing on horses, or your local Junior Academy if competing on ponies. Training schemes for all levels are organized in each area. The full rule book is obtainable from the BSJA at Stoneleigh headquarters.

19 **Trailblazers**

Trailblazers show jumping has rapidly become a very important part of the show-jumping scene in the UK, and is an organization developed to cater for the enthusiastic and more amateur rider. It is sponsored by Spillers, South Essex Insurance Brokers and *Horse* Magazine.

If you want to improve your jumping and competition experience, Trailblazers will give you every opportunity to progress and jump better at whichever level you and your horse are comfortable with. The competition structure is suitable for the true recreational rider with four levels of show-jumping competitions over heights of 75 cm (2 ft 6 in)/85 cm (2 ft 9 in)/95 cm (3 ft 3 in) and 1.05 m (3 ft 6 in), and the competitions are split into Senior and Junior sections.

> **Q** *Are there any restrictions to entries I should be aware of?*
>
> **A** *Yes there are, but they are very minimal and it is unlikely that any of the horses, ponies or riders excluded would want to be competing in Trailblazers.*

Senior classes are open to horses over 14.2 hh and there are no limits on horses' winnings in any of the classes. The only restrictions for Senior riders are that any horse currently registered with the BSJA as Grade A or B may not compete at the finals, and any rider in the top 150 of the BSJA current ranking list is not eligible for the final either.

Junior riders on ponies 14.2 hh and under must not have attained their seventeenth birthday by the first day of the National Championships, and no currently registered JAs (ponies with BSJA winnings of £700 or more) will be permitted to compete at the finals. Riders 13 years and over can ride horses over 14.2 hh in Senior classes on or after their thirteenth birthday.

Approved venues hold the Preliminary Rounds and then all participating riders who have jumped double clear rounds in any or all of their height sections become eligible to go forward and compete in the Second Round or Regional Finals.

Up to this point there have been no membership or registration fees to pay. There is no initial expense, you will just be asked to fill in a membership form at your nearest centre when you first compete. You will be given a one-off membership number and card, and won't have to re-register annually. Once you have qualified by jumping your double clear round in whichever height range you choose to compete, you will be issued with an envelope containing a congratulatory letter telling you that you have qualified at that particular centre. You will then have the choice to either take up the qualification or not. If you wish to accept the qualification for the Second Rounds, you must return the congratulatory letter within 14 days to the centre at which you qualified with a cheque for £12.00.

Remember that this subscription to the Trailblazers organization will only apply if you want to compete in the Second Rounds; it is not compulsory. One Second Round is held at each participating venue, and you may compete in as many Second Rounds as you wish. Four will qualify from each Second Round for the Grand Final to be held at Stoneleigh.

The Trailblazers organizers make this a very special weekend for all the competitors; it is the amateur equivalent to the Festival of Show Jumping or Horse of the Year Show. Top course builders ensure that the arena is dressed immaculately, the classes are organized very professionally, and you are made to feel both special and privileged to be taking part.

Just because you are not jumping huge fences doesn't mean that the competition is not important, and one of the advantages of taking part in Trailblazers is that it will encourage you to progress and improve as and when you wish, from the initial 75 cm (2 ft 6 in) rounds to the Senior or Junior 1.05 Trailblazers Championship.

> **Q** *Are the rules the same as those of the BSJA?*
>
> **A** *Not quite the same, and Trailblazers state simply, 'Jumping rules to apply', without stipulating that they are BSJA rules generally regarded as normal by jumping competitors.*

There is no fine print and some of the penalties mentioned do not concur with current BSJA guidelines. The most obvious difference at the moment is the number of refusals allowed before elimination. Knockdowns receive the same penalties they have always done, i.e. 4 faults, but Trailblazers retain the old BSJA rules for refusals, i.e. 3 faults first refusal, 6 faults second refusal, elimination on third refusal. This is, perhaps, a little kinder and more encouraging than the updated BSJA rules. The BSJA have changed some of these rules and you now receive 4 faults for a first refusal, and are eliminated after a second. A fall of rider or horse incurs elimination in both rule books.

Trailblazers has a far less formal and much shorter rule book than the BSJA and judges are expected to be able to interpret the rules with a bit of common sense. Courses are to be built by a recognized course builder and judged by at least one recognized judge and scorer.

Courses are to consist of a minimum of eight fences including one double, two doubles or one double and a treble. Jump-off courses are to have a minimum of five fences and include one double. The competition tables are similar to the BSJA and are designated very simply.

NT – not timed.

T1 – one round against the clock.

T2 – second round against the clock.

T3 – third round against the clock.

T4 – one round and then if clear immediate jump off against the clock.

> **Q** *Can I go hors concours (non-competitive) and still compete in the same ring afterwards?*
>
> **A** *Yes. Again, this is a kinder and more tolerant ruling than the BSJA hors concours rules.*

Once you have competed *hors concours* at a BSJA show, you may not then enter later classes in the same ring competitively. Trailblazers riders may jump in a class, and their first round is the one that counts for the competition scoring, but they may then elect to go *hors concours* any number of times in that class, as many as the judge will allow. After that, they may then compete in the next class as normal.

This is particularly encouraging for the rider if the horse has taken a dislike to a particular jump. You won't be able to jump better if your horse is allowed to go home triumphantly having succeeded in thwarting your wishes, so the opportunity for extra schooling in a show atmosphere is very welcome.

You will be able to enter and practise over the disliked obstacle properly, even if you have to enter several times, and you will probably find that the judge is sympathetic to your dilemma. It might be expensive on the day because you will have to pay to enter each time you go in the ring, but it will be such a worthwhile exercise as the horse will discover he has no options but to be re-presented at his bogey fence until he gives way. And then you can still take part competitively in the next class.

Q *What tack may I use?*

A *Broadly speaking, anything allowed by the BSJA, but no item of tack may be used inappropriately or in a manner deemed cruel by show director/centre owners.*

Q *What is the Trailblazers dress code?*

A *The dress code is very similar to BSJA guidelines, with a little more latitude regarding your boots and leg wear.*

Hats must be to the maximum current standards and secured at all times whilst riding on the show-ground.

Boots must be black or brown long or jodhpur boots. Gaiters or plain half-chaps (black or brown, no fringes) may be worn with black/brown jodhpur boots. This is slightly more casual than the BSJA which does not allow half-chaps.

Light coloured breeches only.

Hacking or plain-coloured jackets.

Shirts should be white or pastel with a plain tie, stock, or show-jumping collar

Gloves and body protectors are optional.

There is not much difference between the two organizations as far as the less professional rider is concerned except for the cost and the goals. Trailblazers classes are not, at the moment, going to get bigger or more demanding than the 1.05m classes, and the organization has recognized that this is probably the limit for the majority of amateur riders. Once a rider has gained experience in Trailblazers and feels a little more ambitious about jumping bigger fences, they can always join the BSJA as well.

For BSJA members, the new Intro classes fulfil a great need to encourage members to keep jumping and do better but, again, there is little to choose between Intro shows and Trailblazers classes in the size of the courses you will be expected to jump. The real difference is that for more ambitious BSJA members the sky is the limit as there are always more demanding competitions and higher levels to strive for if you wish to. It is no longer necessary to be in the position where you either have to jump bigger or give up membership.

The two organizations are not in opposition but are complementary to each other and so between them they are always going to provide the scope and wherewithal for riders to improve their jumping and progress as far as they are able or inclined.

There is plenty of room in the calendar for them both.

Obviously the BSJA has a long history and all their rules have evolved over a long time. They try to cover every possible eventuality, and are updated constantly. Trailblazers can comfortably use the BSJA guidelines, but may pick and choose or omit some of the rules if they wish to make their organization perhaps a little less formal. Check exactly what the rules and tables are in each Trailblazers class before you compete, you don't want any surprises when things aren't quite the same as the BSJA rule book, although most changes veer to the more lenient side.

The Trailblazers rule book is available from every centre which holds the shows.

Conclusion

I would like to think that *Better Jumping* is relevant in some way for everyone who reads it. If you follow the advice offered and if you are patient and methodical and don't expect any quick fixes or short cuts, you will without fail improve the way you and your horse jump.

I would especially like to thank the riders who allowed me to use unflattering pictures of their efforts as I feel so much can be learned from seeing horse and/or rider performing badly. It doesn't do to gloss over mistakes when practising. If the book were to show everyone performing immaculately all the time it would look good but you are more likely to pick up on some of the less pleasing efforts and recognize that sometimes you may be in exactly that particular situation.

I hope that the advice in the text together with the diagrams and photos, especially of the grid-work exercises, will help you overcome your own problems and encourage and ensure that both you and your horse will enjoy better jumping.